EMBRACING
DIVERSITY

D0057357

To order additional copies of *Embracing Diversity*, by
Leslie N. Pollard, call 1-800-765-6955.
Visit us at *www.rhpa.org* for information on
other Review and Herald products.

EMBRACING
DIVERSITY

How to Understand and
Reach People of All Cultures

LESLIE N. POLLARD, editor

REVIEW AND HERALD® PUBLISHING ASSOCIATION
HAGERSTOWN, MD 21740

This book was
Edited and copyedited by William Cleveland
Designed by Bill Kirstein
Cover illustration by SIS/Randy Verougstraete
Desktop Technician Shirley M. Bolivar
Typeset: 11/13 Garamond Book

PRINTED IN U.S.A.

04 03 02 01 00   5 4 3 2 1

R&H Cataloging Service
Embracing diversity: understanding cultural differences.
    Leslie N. Pollard, ed.

    1. Multiculturalism—Seventh-day Adventist Church.   2. Ethnic relations
3. Race relations.   I. Pollard, Leslie N., ed.

                        306.4

ISBN 0-8280-1543-0

Dedication

This book is dedicated to our world's committed leaders, who risk their lives and careers in working for unity between peoples.

This book is dedicated to our world's teachers, who freely share their accumulated wisdom in the attempt to make us complete people. Your efforts have not been in vain.

This book is dedicated to our world's health-care workers, who freely assist us in our most dire need. You serve without respect to race or creed. We thank you.

This book is dedicated to our world's ministers, who preach the gospel to hurting people in every community. Your efforts have lifted our vision and inspired us to serve God. You have our eternal thanks.

This book is dedicated to our world's young people, who see the future as a day of bright promise.

And, finally, this book is dedicated to our world's children, who show us how to love and play and enjoy the journey called life.

—Leslie N. Pollard
Loma Linda, California

Acknowledgments

A heartfelt thanks to my wife, Prudence, and my daughters, Kristin and Karin, for all of your love and support. This project has required a lot of time away from home. Your understanding and support were indispensable to the preparation of this book.

Also, a very special thanks to Leticia Ortiz, my administrative assistant, who spent long weekend hours typing and retyping the manuscript. Special thanks to Melissa Olmstead, my student worker, for her painstaking transcription of interviews. And I wish to thank especially Ann Bradshaw, a former administrative [assistant?] in the LLU Office of Diversity, who volunteered support time simply because she loves God's diverse people.

Thanks to all the dedicated chapter writers and interviewers, who donated their time and interest because they believe in the global mission of God's international family.

Finally, special thanks to Lyn Behrens, Calvin Rock, and Loma Linda University Board, whose commitment to diversity is exemplary.

Contents

Foreword

At the dawn of time God looked upon His handiwork and said "it was very good" (Genesis 1:31). Embryonically all men and women are merged in that origin. In a sense, we are of each other. Therefore, taken seriously—and is there any other way one can take it?—value statements and opinions that divide mankind ethnically and culturally cannot be sustained. Together we came from the hand of our Maker, and together we have been placed here to realize the potentials of God's design in creation. We walk together and we work together; we play together and we pray together. Together we most surely are. The unavoidable questions are: Shall we love each other, or shall we hate? Shall we build, or shall we destroy?

Hatred and destruction are ultimately suicidal.

There is a future only for the ones who are prepared to move forward into the open space—open society, open opportunities, and open friendships in Christ. He was accused of being a "friend of tax collectors and sinners" (Luke 7:34, NIV). However, in those relationships He was able to communicate joy and belief in both God and the future, and that was very important, for others "in the say" denied these very individuals that sense of an open future with God. These "second class" citizens were made to feel that they were not part of the future, that there was nowhere for them to go to become or to realize their potentials in God. In an exclusive society they did not belong. Christ would have none of it!

That sets the direction and the values for every Christian.

We owe it to God, to humanity and, ultimately, to ourselves to be true to God's design for and value of every human being. Christian leadership can go nowhere else and remain Christian.

—Jan Paulsen, President
General Conference of
Seventh-day Adventists

Introduction

Welcome to the exciting world of leadership in the twenty-first century! *Embracing Diversity* identifies skills for leaders willing to challenge the limitations of the societally imposed boundaries of race, class, culture, gender, and ethnicity. This book will empower leaders to function as visionaries of the new millennium. Its articulation of effective principles, practices, and leader profiles will inspire leaders to lead beyond socially constructed blinders.

If you want to run the race, rather than sit in the stands, *Embracing Diversity* will connect your leadership efforts to vital success skills necessary for leading groups in an interconnected, multicultural world. May we as leaders learn to lead from the inside out, and from the bottom up!

This book is divided into two sections. The first section of the book will help leaders listen to representatives from a variety of ethnic groups describing how their group works, from the inside out. The writers of these chapters describe the values, beliefs, mores, and perspectives that motivate people groups.

The second section of the book presents the strategies used by highly effective diversity leaders. The leaders interviewed have worked with people groups from many different cultures. Their experiences provide a rich resource for effective cross-cultural service.

I have attempted to preserve the individuality of each chapter writer. After all, this book is all about diversity.

Chapter 1

LEADERS, RACE, AND ETHNICITY: TEMPLE OR VEHICLE?

Modern Diversity Questions in the Light of the New Testament

By Leslie N. Pollard

Vice President for Diversity, Loma Linda University
Adventist Health Sciences Center

Changing Demographics and Ethnicity

The world is changing! Demographers say that the world of the twenty-first century will be more globally connected than at any other time in history. Communications technology, media, immigration patterns, educational institutions, and travel are bringing diverse racial and ethnic groups into more intimate association than at any other time in history. "Intensive diversity" is becoming the major descriptor of cross-cultural association in our world. But intensive diversity is not taking place in a vacuum. In every interaction between groups there is a history—sometimes positive; often troubled, tortured; even painful—between people groups that makes cordial cooperation a challenge. This chapter addresses the issue of how Christians can define themselves so that they are a part of the solution, and not the problem.

Race and ethnicity have received substantial attention since the founding of the human family. Historical and biblical documents are replete with tales of tribal, ethnic, and national conflict. While we could cite exceptions, the fact is, throughout human history no society has been free from the contagion of racism and/or ethnocentrism. Racially or ethnically motivated wars, massacres, alienation, "in" group/"out" group oppression—all darken our historical memory. In a fallen world these are the consequences of humanity's sinful propensity to idolize ethnic and racial identity and transform it into something that God never intended. Whether in Kosovo or Bosnia, in Cape Town or Kinshasa, in Jerusalem or the Palestinian West Bank, in Pakistan or India—painful litanies of oppression, genocide, and ethnic cleansing sadden people of conscience. In short, ethnocentrism threatens to short-circuit the best of the human family's community-building efforts.

Definition of Terms Used in This Article

Race refers to a socially constructed category of classification determined by pigmentation, facial features, hair texture, and other biophysical characteristics used to differentiate one group of human beings from others. (By "socially constructed," I mean that in societies it serves a social and legal purpose to have these categories.) In and of itself, the concept of race has no intrinsic worth. And how many races exist among humankind? The number has been as low as three and as high as 22. The concept of race is important only as a means of discussing differences.

Ethnicity refers to a person's personal and social history—how and into which beliefs, values, and worldviews one has been socialized. For instance, my race may be Black, but my ethnicity could be American, Nigerian, Kenyan, or Jamaican. Each of these social contexts influences my outlook on the world.

Racism refers to the belief in the inherent superiority of one race over others, and leads to such practices as discrimination, intolerance, exclusion, and race-based access and privilege.

Ethnocentrism refers to the attitude that one's own ethnic group, nation, or culture is superior to others. From this mind-set emerges the natural tendency to view ethnic differences negatively. This tendency to deny and denigrate differences works to validate and reinforce one's own values and beliefs, a protectionist attitude that seeks to attract and/or preserve privileges and benefits for one's own group.

Ethnocentrism and Its Effect on Society

Consider that the fast-disappearing Ku Klux Klan of the American South could be described as an ethnocentric group. In that group you can observe the following characteristics and outcomes of ethnocentrism.

Ethnocentrism:
- Assumes superiority of a group, clan, tribe, or race.
- Is maintained by resentment of differences.
- Defines itself by clan competition with others.
- Attempts to validate itself by selective comparisons.
- Results in the divinization of the group. Divinization makes the group appear more spiritual, more chosen, more righteous, more privileged, and/or more deserving in the eyes of its members. Adolf Hitler's ethnocentrism is a glaring and tragic example of this phenomenon.

Understandably, the response of leaders of conscience and goodwill to these unfortunate aspects of ethnocentrism, so rife in the world, is the introduction of strategies designed to build community, harmony, and co-operation. This is what the diversity movement is all about. Representing the best and most informed efforts of leaders, both corporate and religious, the diversity movement is intended to capitalize on and maximize the obvious differences between peoples. At the base of secular diversity teaching is a concept called "ethnorelativism."

Ethnorelativism:

- Assumes equality of all groups as one group among many.
- Is informed and maintained by tolerance, openness, and dialogue.
- Defines itself by its ability to level the cultural playing field and promote belonging.
- Attempts to educate groups away from narcissism.
- Results in a moral humanism that promotes harmony between peoples.

The bad news about ethnocentrism and ethnorelativism is that neither contains the power to accomplish their respective objectives. Scripture views ethnocentrism as the group's natural extension of sinful self-centeredness (see Gen. 11:1-8; Rom. 3:11, 12). Thus while some secular authors affirm—and demagogues such as Hitler encouraged—ethnocentrism, it stands condemned in the light of Scripture. The book of Acts and the epistles of Paul and John are explicit rejections of ethnocentrism.

Ethnorelativism, while appealing, falters because humans, as Scripture asserts, are powerless to fully extricate themselves from the hold of their own self-service (see Rom. 1-3; 7:21-25). This is why repeated efforts at peacemaking between peoples are at best fragile and frequently broken. Just ask the United Nations General Assembly.

However, the situation is far from hopeless. God offers a third option. Scripture argues for the primacy and reality of a new value set. Central to the Gospel is the truth that God's grace makes available new possibilities for community and fellowship between different racial and ethnic groups. This chapter presents Scripture's new possibility for managing racial and ethnic identity. Indeed, when Scripture is taken seriously, the matter of how to manage one's racial and ethnic identity becomes crystal clear. Such radical commitment to biblical discipleship will both judge and overcome the numerous "centrisims" put forward by leading social thinkers of the day. The New Testament writer Paul assists us in formulating this new identity in the world. Life in Christ differs from both the ethnocentric and the ethnorelativistic life.

In short, the Christocentric life:

- Assumes fallenness of my group, clan, tribe, race.

- Is maintained by a magnetic attraction to the Christ of the Gospels.
- Defines itself by cooperation with Christ.
- Celebrates self-expenditure on behalf of others.
- Results in a radically new way of viewing and serving others.

This new community (2 Cor. 5:17; Eph. 2:14), organized around Christ, now perceives others differently (verse 16). Observe how Paul instructs us, by word and example, on the appropriate use of racial and ethnic identity:

"For though I be free from all men, yet have I made myself servant unto all, that I might gain the more. And unto the Jews I became as a Jew, that I might gain the Jews; to them that are under the law, as under the law, that I might gain them that are under the law; to them that are without the law, as without law, (being not without law to God, but under the law to Christ,) that I might gain them that are without the law. To the weak became I as weak, that I might gain the weak: I am made all things to all men, that I might by all means save some. And this I do for the gospel's sake, that I might be partaker thereof with you" (1 Cor. 9:19-23). This text gives us a window into Paul's reformulation of racial and ethnic identity.

No doubt we have read this text so frequently that its clear teaching has become obscured. Notice: Paul says, "To the Jews, I became *as* a Jew" (emphasis supplied). Suppose while speaking to African-Americans I said, "To you African-Americans, I become as an African-American." Would someone not say, "But Les, you *are* an African-American"? Well, who was more Jewish than Paul? His racial and ethnic background clearly outline his identity as a Jew of the Jews. "I am an Israelite," he said with some pride, "the seed of Abraham, of the tribe of Benjamin" (Rom. 11:1). "Circumcised the eighth day," he added, "of the stock of Israel, of the tribe of Benjamin, an Hebrew of the Hebrews . . . a Pharisee" (Phil. 3:5).

How, then, can Paul assume this transforming "I become . . ." stance? The answer is in the immediate context. These words come within the stream of Paul's discussion about freedom. The great missionary apostle was given the difficult task of working amid multiple cultures. But Paul labored with great success cross-culturally only and precisely because he was free. His freedom grew out of his encounter with Jesus Christ (see Gal. 1:1). Paul was free from the old "identity anchors" that he once embraced. His identity became grounded in a new experience: "If any man be in Christ, he is a new creation" (2 Cor. 5:17). Thus he could no longer be Judeocentric. This is why he says, "I became as a Jew." Paul no longer considers himself a Jew in terms of primary values, commitments, and allegiance.

The word translated *as* comes from the Greek comparative particle *hos,* which in this verse is the pivotal word. By saying that he became as a Jew, Paul asserts that he *is no longer a Jew.* He is free from the Corinthians because he has not accepted any compensation from them (see verse 15). But because he is free, he is able to enslave himself to people in need of a knowledge of Jesus Christ (see verse 19).

There is no question that the early church was diversity challenged. A quick reading of such texts as Luke 10:30-37; John 4:1-29; Acts 10:17-29; 15:5-10; Galatians 2:7-14; and Ephesians 2:11-19 reveals that the social situation between Jew and Gentile plagued the early church as it attempted to fulfill its mission. As a Jew, Paul felt compelled to persecute the church. That is, until at Damascus Paul received what we might call an "identity transplant" (see Acts 9:1-6). What happened to the racial and ethnic identity that was so visible, so distinguishable, so observable? The answer is in the word "as." The challenge for Christians is to allow the gospel to establish primary identity.

Jan Paulsen, General Conference president, wrote: "Identity is more than 'Where do I come from?' and 'Who are my parents?' It is more than qualification and profession; more than likes and dislikes, smells and tastes. In part, it may be all of the above, but it is the inner reality of my selfhood. My identity is my soul" ("Lessons for Today," *Ministry* magazine, Oct. 1999, p. 4).

First, in the eschatological community (1 Cor. 10:11), race and ethnicity are relocated to a secondary level of identity. Race and ethnicity (and other discreet realities such as gender, class, status, etc.) are no longer the defining realities of our existence. For many secular diversity trainers, primary diversity refers to aspects of identity that one cannot change—race, gender, etc. But in the eyes of the Christian, these social distinctions are "relativized," that is, reduced to what they really are—not objective measures of social worth, but temporal distinctions that are utterly nonsalvific. J. Louis Martyn is correct when he asserts that the encounter with Jesus Christ means the surrender of every "criteria of perception that have been developed apart from the gospel." For Paul, any former or present objectification of race and ethnicity that is not surrendered to Christ becomes idolatry.

Second, as biophysical existence is a gift, with all of its responsibilities, race and ethnicity are endowments to be used, not possessions to be worshiped. Race and ethnicity—those realities in a fallen world that have been used to either marginalize, oppress, classify, denigrate, endow, or privilege—Paul, in this passage, instrumentalizes. His intimate experience as a Jew is vehicularized so that he can be "as" a Jew.

Paul will work for his own racial and ethnic group, but only as an ambassador from another kingdom (2 Cor. 5:20). He adapts himself to the customs of the Jewish people when working among them. He takes a Nazarite vow (Acts 18:18). He has Timothy circumcised (Acts 16:3). He takes part in purification rituals and pays Nazarite expenses for the sacrificial offering (Acts 21:23ff.). But he can also be as one "without the Law," that is, a Gentile. While with Gentiles he does not enforce Jewish ceremonial ritual upon them (Gal. 2:11-14; Col. 2:11, 16), thus laying out the possibility for cross-cultural ministry. Paul works for his "own," but is not limited to them. His ministry is to all people alienated from Jesus Christ.

Third, Paul's motivation is his passion for souls. Love for Christ is the law under which the new Paul functions (1 Cor. 9:21 [see also Gal. 6:2]). His mission is to win as many as possible. Paul's cross-cultural service is motivated by "agape," sacrificial love for others.

Application to the Twenty-first Century

The Christian's encounter with Christ creates both a cross-cultural and a countercultural community. At the cross the church is a repentant community. It is a community that is oriented around the mission of Jesus Christ, as announced in Ephesians 2:14-18. Notice some of its characteristics:

The "cross" cultural community . . .

- Is initiated by the atonement of Jesus Christ.
- Creates a reconciled relationship between groups.
- Destroys hostility.
- Produces peace.
- Redefines personal identity.
- Produces a new center of existence.

While the many centrisms—whether Asiocentrism, Afrocentrism, Eurocentrism, or Latinocentrism—will clamor for our allegiance, the remnant Christian must resist. The gospel never allows believers to organize their perspectives around any other center than Jesus Christ. No person can serve two masters. We can have only one center, Jesus Christ.

While Christian Paul was not Judeocentric, he was deeply Judeo-sensitive. In the same way, as leaders we are not called to be ethnocentric, but to be Christ-centered and ethnosensitive. The first step in this new way of using racial, ethnic, and cultural identity requires an intimate knowledge of one's own racial history and ethnic culture. All of us are ethnic people. We must come to terms with our own personal identity and history, and learn to speak the cultural "language" of our people of origin. By understanding the strengths and weaknesses of the culture and world-view that has been passed on to us, we will be better able to relativize our personal history. This is absolutely essential for the cross-cultural leader.

The second step toward effective cross-cultural leadership requires that we undertake the specific study of the culture of the people whom we lead. Effective missionaries do this all the time. This will require contextually appropriate methods. It may be helpful to consult with persons from the cultures we are serving, to read their history books and find a cultural mentor. Such efforts will be richly rewarded.

A person of any color can provide effective leadership for persons of any other color. Blacks can provide effective leadership for Whites; Whites can provide leadership for Blacks; Hispanics can provide leadership for Whites; Orientals can provide leadership for Blacks; and so on. First Corinthians 9:19-23 implies that every leader is capable of learning to operate effectively beyond her/his base culture.

Conclusion

In a fallen world, race and ethnicity have been sources of separation and alienation. In the church, for the believer, every aspect of our being, including our racial and ethnic identity, can be used as a vehicle for God's service. May God bless your leadership.

Chapter 2

LEADERS AND CROSS-CULTURAL COMMUNICATION: COMMUNICATING ACROSS CULTURAL BOUNDARIES

By Gottfried Oosterwal, Ph.D., Litt.D.

Professor and Director Emeritus,
Center for Intercultural Relations, Andrews University

Communication is the sharing of messages with the least possible distortions. These distortions are, of course, inevitable. Within a leader's own culture, they are the result of differences in age and gender, social status and economic background, race and ethnicity, education and religion, personality factors and personal experiences, between the *sender* (S) and the *receiver,* or *respondent* (R). As a result, only about 45-60 percent of all communication within one's own culture is effective. In a cross-cultural setting, however, that percentage is only 20-25 percent! This low rate of effectiveness—that is, of communication that is clear and undistorted, without misunderstandings and misinterpretation—is the result of the differences created by *culture.*

It is important to stress here that these cultural differences are not shaped by biophysical factors such as race or color of the skin, nor are they external and material, such as the way people dress or eat or walk or behave. They are rooted in differences in values, in people's basic cultural assumptions, in the way they perceive reality, and in their views of what is right or wrong, good or bad, ideal and desirable. These constitute the layers that shape the dynamics of the process of communication between *sender* (S) and *recipient* (R) (see graph), and, in addition to the layers of age and gender, etc., are responsible for the misunderstandings and distortions and misinterpretations that are characteristics of all cross-cultural communication.

Can these differences be reduced or overcome? Is effective cross-cultural communication possible? To both questions the answer is a resounding yes! And one of the hallmarks of a great leader in a multicultural setting is that he or she has a deep awareness of, and sensitivity toward, these differences, and has mastered the basic principles of cross-cultural communication.

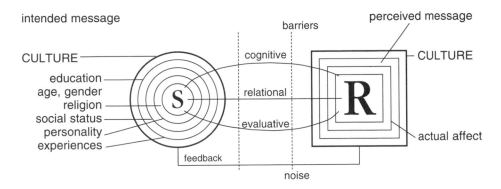

Basic Principles of Cross-Cultural Communication

Though it may seem at first that all humans communicate in the same way physically and physiologically, it is culture that even shapes the very nature of communication. In North America, for instance, and in northern Europe, the aim of communication is "getting the message across"; "sharing information"; "proclaiming the truth"; "making the point." And that is achieved on the *cognitive* level of communication: using rational arguments and appealing to people's rational understanding by way of words, orally or in writing, eye-to-eye or on the phone, by fax, or by e-mail.

In most other cultures, however, the aim of communication is not, in the first place, "to get the message across" or "to inform." It is what the term *communication* already suggests: to *establish a communion;* to create a bond, a (new) relationship. Information is also shared, but only after, or as part of, establishing a bond, a fellowship, or a communion. That's why leaders from, say, North America or Europe so often do not get their point across in areas where building relationships are primary, and the sharing of information comes second.

In Mexico or in Japan, for example, they say, "We don't do business with strangers," thereby implying that a relationship must be established before messages can be sent or heard. Here communication starts and is based on the "relational level." The Chinese express this in their notion to all effective communication. In the Philippines it is called *pakik-isama,* that warm, interpersonal relationship without which there is no effective sharing of information. In Indonesia it is called *gotong royong,* which in Singapore is actually the basis of the social structure and all human interactions.

In all of these cultures—and these are the majority in the world—

merely delivering a message, or even *"the message,"* remains without effect unless a relationship has first been established. This militates against just flying in one day, delivering the message or conducting business, and flying out the next.

In many cultures, moreover, communication is also shaped powerfully by the *evaluative level:* the way the sender dresses or behaves, the speaker's poise and style. When an American union conference president opened a General Conference session in the United States dressed in cowboy boots and a ten-gallon Stetson—to set the tone—he was greeted by joyful applause and laughter by people from his own culture. But he was totally misunderstood and, therefore, rejected by delegates from cultures in which communication is more formal.

"Cannot you American leaders take anything seriously?" was the most-often-heard remark. The message was not even heard, and the hearers were shocked in their dignity, and what was considered the dignity of the event. Culturally aware leaders avoid the often casual and informal poise loved in American culture when communicating in a multicultural setting and in cultures that are far more formally organized and structured.

Leadership Keys

What, then, are those basic principles of cross-cultural communication, and how can leaders of a multicultural organization master them? For brevity's sake, they can be summarized under five main headings.

1. Words do not have meaning by themselves; words derive their meaning from people's underlying cultural assumptions, values, and perceptions. Take the word "boy." In general, it stands for a male child and often has the connotation of endearment and familiarity ("good old boy"). In the African-American culture, however, it has an utterly negative meaning. It's a patronizing term, with racial overtones, insulting and offensive. The meaning of a word is not determined by that word itself, but by the underlying cultural assumptions and perceptions associated with it. That's why "all dictionaries are liars."

One day, as part of an assignment for his English class, a professor at Andrews University required his students to write a report on the sermon to be given during the Sabbath worship hour. His three students from the People's Republic of China were unable to produce the required report. Their reason? "We went to church, all right, but we did not understand one word. The message did not make sense."

These three students spoke English very well. But the words used in the sermon conveyed a meaning they did not understand. They heard them through the layers of their own Chinese and Communist culture. Words such as liberation and salvation, church and power, struggle and freedom, in their hearing have totally different meanings from those conveyed in our American Christian setting. And so do ordinary words such as family, friend, cousin, or numbers and colors. The number 4 in Chinese culture is a symbol of death. And so is the color white! Red, on the other hand, is perceived as the symbol of happiness and well-being; whereas in other cultures that color stands for evil and sinfulness: "Though your sins are . . . red as crimson, they shall be like wool" (Isa. 1:18, NIV).

Dr. Martin Luther King, Jr., maintained that "our own [American] culture conspires against us [Blacks]." Consulting a thesaurus, he found 130 different meanings and shades of meanings of the word *white,* all positive: good, pure, clean, innocent, holy, etc. Yet among the 120 entries for *black* he found only one with a positive meaning. All others were negative: evil, death, inferior, dirty, sad, wicked, dismal, etc, as in blackmail, black market, blacklisting, etc. Words don't stand on their own; they derive meaning from their underlying cultural assumptions and perceptions.

Take the word *grace,* the very core of the Christian gospel. In the Philippines it is translated *biyaya,* which literally means "gift," a similar shade of meaning as in biblical Greek. But the cultural assumptions and values associated with that concept give *biyaya,* grace, its specific meaning.

Philippine culture, like a majority of cultures in Africa, Asia, and Latin America, is rooted in the value of *reciprocity.* Unlike in the United States, where a gift is a one-way movement free of any obligations on the part of the recipient, a gift, a *biyaya,* in cultures rooted in reciprocity resembles a two-way street: the gift requires, it obligates, the recipient to give something in return. Without fulfilling that obligation, that duty, there exists a broken relationship between giver and receiver. *Biyaya* (grace, gift) has the connotation of God obligating the recipient to give something in return in order for the relationship to be perfected. And vice versa—any gift given to God requires Him to give something in return, such as blessings, protection, forgiveness.

The concept is not unbiblical. Reciprocity is a key value in Hebrew culture. "If you [Israel; a person] do this, I, God, will do that." You can test me, says God. Malachi 3:8-12 is only one example among many. But people hearing the Gospel message in the context of the cultural value of reciprocity, can not clearly hear or experience the message of God's grace. Unless the cross-cultural communicator is aware of this value and adjusts his message accordingly.

Leaders who are aware of this first principle of cross-cultural communication will not take their messages or sermons prepared for a European or North American audience and deliver them in the same way and form in other cultures. They will make themselves aware of these underlying values and assumptions shaping the recipients' hearing and understanding. They will sit also beforehand with their translator and go over the meaning of the words to be used, and they will allow the translator to "ad lib" freely in order to explain the message. They will also take plenty of time to first establish a relationship before sharing the message or conducting business.

2. Consider not only the content of the message, but also its context. Anthropologists make a distinction between so-called *high-context cultures* and *low-context cultures.* Northern European cultures, and those of Canada, the United States, Australia, and New Zealand, are (very) low-context cultures. Those, on the other hand, of Mexico, the Philippines, Kenya, and Japan are high-context cultures.

In low-context cultures, communication is *direct;* it uses few words. "Anything worth saying," the Dutch say, "can be said short." A sick patient there, asking his physician whether the disease is serious, will get a straight answer: "Yes" or "No." A physician in a high-context culture will typically respond to that question like this: "When I was a little girl, I had an aunt. Her name was Emilia. She was married to a man from the Bicol Province. Now, in the Bicol Province you'll find the most perfectly shaped volcano, Mount Mayon . . ."

A person from a low-context culture, hearing this answer, will think, *I am about to die; she does not want to tell me; she's beating around the bush.* Wrong! Communication in high-context cultures is through an often-artistic flow of words and a lot of "loopings" and "detours." It is through concrete examples, rather than by the use of abstract terms; it is through stories and parables.

A well-known corporate leader from the United States, conducting a series of meetings in Kenya, East Africa, blundered terribly when, shortly before a vote would be taken (a rather low context way of conducting business!), he consented to let a gentleman from Kenya make a "last-minute" statement.

To make his point, the African gentleman began, "When I was a boy, we were not very rich." He paused. "We were not very poor either. We had 12 goats. The name of the first goat is . . . The name of the second goat is . . . The name of the third goat is . . ."

At that point the American leader could no longer restrain himself, thinking of all the time being "wasted" by the man "not coming to the point." He interrupted the speaker and rather angrily shouted, "Please, come to the point, sir!"

The gentleman from Kenya sat down, feeling terribly insulted and offended. He had been making his point all along by implication and analogies, precisely and concretely. There is meaning in the name of a goat. The parable of the goat was the message, it was the point! The man from the Western culture had no idea. He did not get the point, being unfamiliar with the notion of communication in high-context cultures, in which one "makes the point" through parables and stories, through personal experiences, concretely, and not in abstract terms. Is not this the way Jesus communicated with people? Surely, that lesson should not elude us.

Among other powerful differences between communication in high and low-context cultures are *proxemics:* the distance between sender and receiver. This distance is defined spatially, but also in status: *hierarchical* versus *democratic, eye-contact* (a form of disrespect in many high-context cultures), and *touching* (in general, forbidden in low-context cultures).

Low-context cultures, moreover, are highly *time-conscious* and extremely *task-oriented* ("Get the job done, quickly"). They also are *information-focused.* High-context cultures, on the other hand, are *person-oriented.* It's not time that counts; it's the *event* that is important. High-context cultures focus on *relationships* first, and consider the message second. The apostle Paul admonished us to "speak the truth in love" (Eph. 4:15, NEB), that is, embedded in, and as part of, a warm, personal friendship relation, an environment of love.

Finally, low-context cultures are *individuals-oriented;* whereas high-context cultures speak and hear, send and receive, all messages in the context of the group, the family, the community. There, decisions too are made, not as individuals, independent of others, but interdependent with others, as part of a group.

Leaders aware of these contextual differences will not address the audience as "my friends," or make an appeal to individual hearers. People in high-context cultures hear and respond in groups, interdependent with others making the same decisions.

3. Every culture has its own mode of communication. During communication, should a sender present the message in a rational way, devoid of emotions, low-keyed, dispassionate, through symbols, impersonal, with an emphasis on the task, or the message, or the product? Or would the sharing of the message become more effective by utilizing animated and argumentative engagement; by being passionate, dynamic, emotional, challenging, assertive, people-oriented; by taking sides and calling for responses?

In most low-context cultures, the sender communicates in the first mode: using words sparingly, low-key, with few if any gestures, and without detours and personal emotions. Many of these characteristics, however, are also found in a number of otherwise high-context cultures, such as Japan or China.

Similarly, aspects of the second mode of communication can also be found in a number of low-context cultures. Mode and context of communication are distinct aspects of the process. Take, for example, African-American communication in the United States. Though African-Americans do share in the generally low-context culture of the United States, their mode of communication, unlike that of the Anglo-White population, is high-keyed: animated, confrontational, intense, and assertive; argumentative; passionate and affective; dynamic and emotional; challenging and struggling (see appendix). For that reason, a special course is offered in the Seventh-day Adventist Theological Seminary on "Black preaching." And rightly so. Black American leaders, however, need to realize that when communicating with European (White) audiences, this mode, so powerful in their own culture, often makes their communication ineffective, sometimes insulting.

The same is true for the Anglo-White mode for African-American audiences; it comes across as boring, impersonal, cold, hypocritical, devious, uninvolved. Like cultures as a whole, these modes of communication are not determined by biophysical factors. There are racially and ethnically White cultures in South America or in southern Europe, where the mode of communication is highly animated, emotional, with many gestures and the use of facial expressions. And there are racially and ethnically Black cultures in Africa and in Melanesia, where communication is unemotional, low-keyed, with long periods of silence, restrained, detached, etc.

Culturally aware leaders will know how to deliver their message, and in which mode. And no leader will try to impose his or her own culturally defined mode of communication upon audiences or institutions of other cultures, or consider it superior or more effective than the other.

Too many mistakes are being made that way. There really is not just one best and most effective way of doing evangelism, of conducting business meetings, of sharing the message, of worship!

4. Always keep in mind the true purpose of communication. Article 2 of the constitution of the General Conference of Seventh-day Adventists describes "the purpose of the General Conference" as "to teach all nations the everlasting gospel of our Lord and Saviour Jesus Christ and the commandments of God. That statement reflects beautifully and powerfully the North American culture's purpose of communication: "to teach," "to inform," "to proclaim," "to make known."

In biblical culture, as well as in the majority of cultures outside of North America, Europe, Australia, and New Zealand, that purpose is defined in the first place as "establishing a relationship; creating a bond, a communion, a fellowship." In terms of Scripture: "to bring about reconciliation"; to establish a new communion, the body of Christ; to make people disciples, followers of Christ.

In these cultures, the sharing of information (the teaching of truths) is also taking place, but as part of, and embedded in, the greater and overall goal of establishing a (new) communion between sender and receiver. In fact, it is that (biblical) emphasis in these cultures on that purpose and goal of establishing a relationship, a communion, that contributes greatly to their effectiveness in mission and evangelism and church growth.

Recently, at the Rose Bowl Parade in Pasadena, California, a Christian group participated with their beautiful float. Messengers, dressed as angels proclaimed through mighty loudspeakers that God is for real, that His Word should be obeyed, and that people ought to repent of their sins and accept the Lord Jesus Christ as their Saviour. A few weeks later this church group's publication announced in glowing terms that on that day "the gospel had been communicated to over 2 million people." Had it been? Yes, in terms of our culture's purpose of communication: to teach, to make known, to inform.

But from another cultural perspective, including the biblical one, had people become reconciled to God? Had a new fellowship been established, a new communion with God? In biblical terms, the sender of the message is as the One who sends him or her! Culturally aware leaders must be aware of the differences between their own cultural ways and those of others, and then make the necessary adjustments. They also must have the courage to recognize where their own cultural understanding falls short.

All cultures have their shortcomings and limitations, including our very own! At that point, leadership in a multicultural setting demands that we learn from others, and make it our own. The whole purpose of communication is a powerful case in point. In fact, the lack of effectiveness in evangelism and mission in the Anglo-White cultures of Europe, North America, Australia, and New Zealand (in spite of their technological advances) is, to a large extent, a result of the culturally determined purpose of communication as "teaching," "informing," "making known," and "proclaiming," with their obvious limitations. Culturally aware leaders will learn from other cultures that the real purpose of communication is to establish communion between people, to bring about a new community, to create a new bond, a new fellowship.

Is that not also the very core of biblical communication? The Great Commission of Matthew 28:18-20 really reads: "As you are going out everywhere to make disciples, teach them, baptize them, tell them . . ." The true purpose for which the church exists is to make disciples, to bring about reconciliation, to establish a new communion.

5. There is no communication without identification. At this point, one more aspect of the purpose of communication needs to be considered: the way in which this new communion between people can be established. The key term here is *identification.* As we learn from the social and the communication sciences, there is no communication without identification! What that means, in practice, is that in order for a message—or *the message*—to be clearly understood and accepted, the sender must identify with the recipients, become one with them in the setting of their particular culture, empathize with them, declare himself or herself in solidarity with them.

This does not mean giving up one's own ideals and values, or compromising the truths entrusted to the sender. What it does mean is that those truths and values and messages must be heard and seen and experienced in forms and modes and values and symbols of the recipients' own culture. And that will happen when the sender, as a person or as an institution, takes on those forms and modes and values and symbols of the other culture in fellowship and communion with its people. Is that not what we learn also from the apostle Paul, who, in all his communication across cultural boundaries, stressed this point of identification as the core of all effective communication: becoming a Greek with the Greeks, a Roman with the Romans; becoming one with the people in a new solidarity and fellowship.

The apostle writes in 1 Corinthians 9:19-23: "I have made myself a

slave to all, that I might win the more. . . . I became a Jew, in order to win
the Jews; to those under the law I became as one under the law—though
not being myself under the law—that I might win those under the law. To
those outside the law I became as one outside the law—not being without
law toward God but under the law of Christ—that I might win those outside the law. To the weak I became weak, that I might win the weak. I
have become all things to all men, that I might by all means save some. I
do it all for the sake of the gospel, that I may share in its blessings" (RSV).

Here is that "great communicator," Paul, who traversed the world of
his day, communicating the message to that world by crossing all kinds
of cultural boundaries through the act of *identification,* and for the sole
purpose of "saving people" and "reconciling them to God."

Ellen G. White, using the apostle Paul as her model, stresses the same
in her writings, in particular in her *Gospel Workers,* a book written for
the explicit purpose of helping leaders to communicate the message
across cultural boundaries.

But rather than merely looking at these powerful principles of cross-
cultural communication in the light of the sciences, or as illustrated by
mission history, or as part of current practices of effective church
growth, let us consider the whole issue of communicating across cultural
boundaries. The answer is clearly given in the sending of His Son, Jesus
Christ. God could have shouted the message of His gospel from the heav-
ens, and everyone would have heard it. He could have written the message with His finger in the sky. He could have sent His angels to proclaim
it and have it accompanied with plagues and catastrophes. In fact, God
did all that.

In the end, though, God chose the way of *identification:* He became
as one of us: poor with the poor, an Asian with the Asians. He took upon
Himself our existence, our culture.

The Incarnation is the basis of all effective cross-cultural communication: becoming one with the people, taking on their cultural ways for the
express purpose of establishing a new relationship with God, a new fellowship, a new communion. This is the purpose of all cross-cultural
communication.

For further reading:

Jandt, Fred E. *Intercultural Communication: An Introduction.* Thousand
    Oaks, Calif.: Sage Publication, 1999.

Oosterwal, Gottfried. *Community in Diversity: A Workbook.* Berrien Springs, Mich.: Center for Intercultural Relations, 1999.

Smith, Donald K. *Creating Understanding: A Handbook for Christian Communication Across Cultural Landscapes.* Grand Rapids, Mich.: Zondervan, 1997.

Chapter 3

LEADERSHIP INSIGHTS FOR ASIANS IN THE TWENTY-FIRST CENTURY

By Won Yoon, Ph.D.

Assistant to the President,
Professor of Sociology, LaSierra University

I need to make a few assumptions to delimit the scope of this chapter. First, this chapter is mainly for Westerners interested in Asian culture (in both a geographical and a cultural sense, Asia is referred to as "the East," in contrast to Europe and the United States, which are referred to as "the West").

Second, whenever I use the words *Asian culture,* I am referring to the somewhat distinctive traditional cultural traits of Asian peoples. A typical Asian can be expected to think and behave differently from his or her Western counterpart in any given circumstance. Such an assumption is necessary as Asia is changing rapidly under such banners as development, modernization, industrialization, Westernization/Americanization, internationalization, globalization, and the like. As a result, the difference between East and West is becoming increasingly blurred, especially among Asian young people.

Finally, the collective term *Asians* refers to the peoples living in the countries along the Asian Pacific Rim (formerly the Far Eastern Division), including China, Japan, Korea, Vietnam, Thailand, and other countries of Southeast Asia.

Facts About Asia

Before we narrow down our discussion on the countries and peoples of the Pacific Rim, an overview of the entire Asian continent is helpful in understanding the contrasts that exist between the cultures of the Pacific Rim nations and the Asian continent, and between Asia and the world.

Among the six continents of the world, Asia is the largest in terms of land mass, covering nearly one third of the earth's land area. The vast continent stretches some 6,000 miles (9,600 kilometers) from east to west and 5,400 miles (8,640 kilometers) from north to south—the largest Asian country, China, can be squarely juxtaposed on the American continent proper.

Sixty percent of the world's population inhabits the Asian continent (the peoples of China and India alone account for almost 40 percent of the world's population). The sheer size of Asia is matched only by the diversity of its geography and cultures.

Asia may be divided into five regional and cultural areas: Northeast Asia (China, Japan, Korea, etc.), Southeast Asia (Indonesia, the Philippines, Vietnam, etc.), South Asia (India, Pakistan, Sri Lanka, etc.), Central Asia (Afghanistan, Kazakhstan, Uzbekistan, etc.), and the Middle East (Israel, Kuwait, Saudi Arabia, etc.). More than 40 sovereign nations occupy the map of Asia, and inhabitants from the Arctic tundra (Siberia) to the tropical rain forests of Indonesia speak almost 400 languages and dialects.

Considered the cradle of ancient civilization, the Asian continent gave birth to the Chinese civilization along the Yellow River, the Indian civilization along the Ganges and Indus Rivers, and the Mesopotamian civilization along the Euphrates and Tigris Rivers. Also, all major world religions originated in Asia and have had an enormous impact on those regions in which they have been dominant: the Middle East and Central Asia by Islam, the subcontinent of India by Hinduism and Buddhism, Southeast Asia by Buddhism and Islam, and Northeast Asia by Buddhism and Confucianism. At present, Christianity is strong in South Korea and the Philippines.

Asia is a vastly diverse continent, thus one should avoid any sweeping generalizations and be specific in your references to Asia, Asian peoples, and their culture.

For the successful cross-cultural leader, it is helpful to . . .

- Understand the roots of Asian pride in terms of its size, ancient civilizations, and long history.
- Acknowledge the contribution of Asia to the civilization of humankind through religion and other achievements.
- Be aware of the considerable intra-Asian prejudices among the regions and nations.

Asian Encounters With the West: A Historical Example of China

China, even before the time of Jesus, was linked with the Roman Empire through the 4,000-mile "silk road," the route traveled to exchange goods between Asia and Europe. The first European to step on Chinese soil was John de Plano Carpini, a Franciscan friar, in 1246; then Venetian

34

merchant brothers Nicolo and Maffeo Polo in 1264; and Nicolo's son, Marco Polo, in 1275. The first Jesuit missionary assigned to China, Matteo Ricci, landed in the Middle Kingdom in 1582.

As Western commercial interests and political influence grew in China, the clash resulted in the infamous Opium Wars of the mid-1800s. Around this time other Asian countries became colonies of Western nations (the return of Macau to China on December 20, 1999, is symbolic in that it marks the end of European imperial presence in Asia).

Like China, most Asian countries were forced to open up to the West through the "three M's": *merchants, missionaries,* and the *military.* And their objectives were the "three G's": *gold,* the *gospel,* and the *glory* of their nations. Western missionaries, in spite of their noble religious motivations, were perceived by some Asian rulers as part of a Western plot to conquer Asia.

Today the attitude of Chinese and other Asian peoples—particularly the older generation—to Westerners has been shaped by the historical experiences of their forefathers in the past two centuries. Suspicion, resistance, and hostility toward Westerners reflect these Asians' knowledge of the past history of the continent. At the same time, Asians' desire to claim the next century as the "Asian century" or the "Pacific century" may be looked upon as their wish to counteract the humiliation of the centuries of domination by Western nations.

For the successful cross-cultural leader, it is helpful to . . .

- Understand the xenophobic attitude of Asian peoples in the former European colonies in the context of their historical experiences.
- Avoid any appearance of superiority and dominance in dealing with Asians.
- Be careful in presenting yourself as a missionary or religious leader to Asians who are not Christians.
- Attempt to find common ground between the teachings of Christianity and other Asian religions; take an integrated approach.
- Regard your Asian counterparts as equals.

Asian Cultural DNA

Although most Asian countries along the Pacific Rim have shown rapid change since the end of World War II, mainly in the direction of Westernization/Americanization, there are certain cultural elements that define Asian peoples. For the purpose of this chapter, a few deeply ingrained cultural elements, what Professor Tu Wei-ming of Harvard

University called cultural DNA, are highlighted: the family, filial piety, formality, education, honor, and self-control among others. In general, the origin of these cultural elements can be traced back to the influences of Confucian teachings.

Family

Asians typically regard the family as the first, central, and lasting social entity, and their lives, identity, and social standing are closely associated with this most basic institution. From ancient times the ideal family has been characterized by harmony and order, and harmony and order are maintained by clearly defined hierarchical relationships and gender and age roles in the family.

Thus, the nature of family interaction is shaped by status, and status is determined largely by age, gender, generation order, and marital status—the older over the younger, the male over the female, the preceding generation over the subsequent generation, and the married over the unmarried. Knowing one's place and behaving accordingly, therefore, is very important in establishing the predictable manner of relationships among family members that assures harmony and order. There is a saying that "peace in the family makes everything possible."

Often individual happiness is given up for family harmony. In the traditional Asian family, individual rights and space are not given a high priority, and privacy in both the physical and the psychological sense is a relatively recent concept. It is less known among subordinate members of the family, whose submission is unquestioned. For this reason, the virtues of obedience and patience are highly emphasized.

Asian families tend to be closed to outsiders in both a physical and a social sense. Most houses, for instance, are enclosed by high walls, with only the roofs visible; outsiders are seldom invited in. For this reason, tea houses, cafes, restaurants, and karaoke chambers are popular venues for meetings and other social functions.

Asian children are punished by being forced to stay away from their homes, while American children are punished by being grounded at home. The former punishment involves the removal of one's sense of home security, and the latter, the restriction of one's freedom of movement.

Families (both consanguine and conjugal) presuppose homogeneity, and this has increased Asians' concern with the homogeneity of their societies, and more specifically, their common ancestry, social standing, language, expectations and conduct, and geographical boundaries.

Actually, the modern version of the extended Asian family has come to include corporations and even the state. In Chinese, for instance, the word for country consists of two characters: nation and family. For this reason, Asian politicians and organizational leaders often behave like benevolent parents, expecting trust and loyalty from their followers.

For the successful cross-cultural leader, it is helpful to . . .

- Understand that Asians tend to view most human relations in terms of family relations, and that trust is an important element.
- Recognize that the concept of the extended family is more likely to lead to the formation of cliques along the lines of clan, birthplace, and school affiliation.
- Take into consideration the fact that Western concepts of checks and balances in public life are not fully developed, thus creating environments that are more conducive to irregularity.
- Realize that in hierarchical human relations, the superordinate is expected to behave benevolently and the subordinate submissively.
- Recognize that Asians' tendency to be exclusive to outsiders might be rooted in the concept of the closed family.
- Accept substantial resistance to egalitarian relationships between different ages, genders, and organizational positions.
- See that sacrifice for the common good is expected of group members.

Filial Piety

Perhaps no other concept is more crucial to the understanding of the Asian mind-set than filial piety. The core of Asian family relations, filial piety, the affection, respect, and obligation children exhibit toward their parents, forms the foundation for Asian ethics. Filial piety actually continues in the form of ancestral worship after the parents have passed away.

Ideally speaking, filial piety is derived from the children's profound sense of indebtedness to their parents for their very birth and life. Suffering and hardship incurred by parents for their children are to be reciprocated. Anyone who fails to pay back this indebtedness to his or her parents is looked upon with contempt.

Filial piety, in fact, extends beyond the parent-child relationship to one's teacher, superior, and ruler. This, to some extent, explains why Asians are sometimes profuse in their expressions of gratitude and gift-giving.

For the successful cross-cultural leader, it is helpful to . . .

- Reciprocate in maintaining human relationships. Be conscious about expressing gratitude to your Asian counterparts.

- Not misread a kind offer or an unexpected gift for an inappropriate motivation.
- Recognize that "going Dutch" is seldom practiced among acquaintances. Obligation may begin with inferiors (students for teachers, church members for their pastors), but should be reciprocated by superiors as an expression of generosity.

Formality

Compared to Westerners, Asians exhibit a formality in manners and speech that should be understood in the context of the vertical human relationships common to Asian family settings and beyond. This formality is designed to achieve social order, which is maintained by status distinction and conformity. Enforcement of different role responsibilities and conformity requires the authority of superiors. Thus the proper public presentation of oneself is a challenging task if one is not familiar with the intricacies of formality and protocol.

In some Asian languages, both nouns and verbs reflect these different levels, known as "honorific layers." One must select the proper honorific level according to the age and social status of the other person. Violation of this rule can be embarrassing and often offensive.

Even in casual social gatherings, most Asian adults call each other by surnames. In a public gathering, they never refer to one another by first or given names. Brother/Sister Yamamoto, Elder/Pastor Vien, or Dr./Union President Lee are utilized. This formality is, in a sense, a distinction-maintaining device, and distinction is maintained by distance, both physical and social.

For the successful cross-cultural leader, it is helpful to . . .

- Be rather formal in your dress and speech if you are not sure whether informality is proper. Being casual or informal is still a foreign concept among many Asians.
- Call your host by his or her surname unless your counterpart is very close to you or is educated in America.
- Be careful of making physical contact in public with your Asian hosts; it is better to avoid such contact even with your spouse.

Honor

Upholding respect in the eyes of others is a very serious matter. In a conformity-oriented society, having the approval of others is an important aspect of social life. Bringing shame upon one's name, on the other hand, is an unbearable social stigma. For this reason, ridicule is a powerful means of controlling the behavior of people. Sometimes one's failure to meet the expectations of others—that is, losing face—may result in tragedy. A student who fails an entrance exam, a leader who fails at his leadership role, and a spouse who commits a shameful act may resort to suicide. They choose such an extreme measure because suicide is looked upon as an honorable act to save face.

For the successful cross-cultural leader, it is helpful to . . .
- Treat others with respect and dignity in speech and manners.
- Avoid, if possible, causing embarrassment by pointing out someone's mistakes and shortcomings in public.
- Not apply Western-style individualistic thinking.
- Understand Asians' concern for the opinion of others.

Education

Besides the ascribed positions traditionally determined by age, gender, and family rank, honor derives from the social position one achieves. In traditional Asian society, that honor is achieved mainly through learning. For instance, in China the highest prestige was given to scholars who were well versed in literature and history. High government officials were selected through a civil service exam until the turn of the twentieth century. Interestingly, wealthy merchants and craftspersons were regarded much lower in social prestige than poor scholars. Confucius said that nothing in life is superior to learning. The impressive economic growth of the Pacific Rim countries may be attributed, in large measure, to the tradition of socially valuing learning.

For the successful cross-cultural leader, it is helpful to . . .
- Be aware that one's educational background, both in quantity and prestige, is an important social factor in determining one's social position.
- Be well prepared in terms of knowledge and information when working with Asians. Often their evaluation of your ability as a leader or colleague might be based on your command of your area of expertise.
- Show a genuine interest in promoting education whenever such a topic is relevant.

Self-control

Westerners tend to stereotype Asians as lacking expression. Classic

Asian paintings tend to support such an impression, because in many paintings, the human faces portrayed do not convey emotion. Even in modern-day family photographs, one cannot easily determine the actual feelings of the subjects because of the lack of facial expression.

This tendency to a lack of emotional expression is related to the value Asians hold for the virtue of self-control, considered the mark of a cultivated person or a scholar, or in Japanese society, the Samurai culture. Only immature people, such as children, express emotion, because they cannot help it. Thus it is sometimes difficult to read an Asian's state of mind as his or her inner feelings are seldom revealed in words and body language.

As direct and open expressions of feeling are shunned, subtle euphemism is a tactic adopted by many. However, unless one is familiar with the context under which such interaction takes place, it is not easy to figure out the intent of the communicators. Thus, resulting from the straightforward and open communication style that they employ, many Westerners experience difficulties in their dealings with Asians.

For the successful cross-cultural leader, it is helpful to . . .

- Make an effort to figure out the hidden meanings in verbal communication.
- Do not misread the lack of expression of Asian counterparts for a lack of feeling.
- Avoid confrontational approaches, if possible, that may cause a loss of face.

Conclusion

You might be surprised at how Western many Asians are, especially the young and those who have traveled extensively or been educated in Western countries. Nonetheless, certain cultural elements are deeply ingrained regardless of educational background and life experiences. The aspects presented in this chapter may be used as guidelines in your relationships with a variety of Asians, ranging from ultratraditional to highly Westernized.

For further reading:

Benedict, Ruth. *The Chrysanthemum and the Sword: Patterns of Japanese Culture.* Tokyo: Charles E. Tuttle Co., 1989.

Borthwick, Mark. *Pacific Century: The Emergence of Modern Pacific Asia.* Boulder, Colo.: Westview Press, 1992.

Cameron, Nigel. *From Bondage to Liberation: East Asia 1860-1952.* Hong Kong: Oxford University Press, 1975.

Clyde, Paul H. and Burton F. Beers. *The Far East: A History of Western Impacts and Eastern Responses, 1830-1975.* Englewood Cliffs, N.J.: Prentice-Hall, 1975.

Videotapes:

A Confucian Life in America: Tu Wei-ming. Films for the Humanities, Inc.

Between Two Worlds. University of California Extension.

Doubles: Japan and America's Intercultural Children. Regge Life.

The Coming of the Barbarians (1540-1650). Films for the Humanities, Inc.

Chapter 4

LEADERSHIP INSIGHTS FOR AFRICANS IN THE TWENTY-FIRST CENTURY

By Baraka G. Muganda, D.Min.

Youth Director, General Conference of Seventh-day Adventists

Africa, the second largest of the world's seven continents, covers about 11,699,000 square miles (30,330,000 square kilometers), including its adjacent islands. In 1990 about 12 percent of the world's population, an estimated 642 million people, lived in Africa, making it the world's second most populous continent after Asia.

This great continent is home to many of the world's great ancient civilizations, including the Egyptian empire, which achieved domination more than 5,000 years ago. However, the past 500 years in Africa have been dominated by foreign colonization and political and ethnic struggles that have hampered modern industrial and social development.

Beginning in the early sixties, though, African nations began to gain independence from their former colonial powers. And with independence came basic societal changes, including the introduction of multiparty democratic governments and greater efforts to educate their populations.

Peoples indigenous to the African continent are believed to be the most culturally diverse of any in the world. In fact, Africa boasts more that 3,000 distinct ethnic groups. Black Africans make up the majority of the continent's population, but there are also large populations of Arabs, Asians, Europeans, and Berbers.

More than 1,000 languages are spoken in Africa, making the continent linguistically diverse. Though the majority of these languages are spoken by relatively few people, more than 50 languages have 500,000 or more speakers each. Apart from French and English, the most widely spoken languages are Swahili, Hausa, and Arabic. Many Africans, particularly those of the Sub-Saharan region, are bilingual, speaking their own language as well as that brought by earlier European colonial administrations.

Christianity, Africa's most widespread religion, was introduced into

Northern Africa in the first century and spread to the Sudan and Ethiopian regions in the fourth century. Christianity survived in Ethiopia principally through the Coptic Church. However, in the other areas Christianity was swept away by Islam. Christianity was reintroduced and spread through tropical Africa with the fifteenth-century rise of European overseas expansion. Today Protestantism and Catholicism are about equally represented throughout the continent.

Leadership Keys

1. Understand tribes. Africa has a highly developed system of tribal belonging. Tribal membership, in fact, forms the basis of one's identity, and Africans have a deep pride in their tribes. Countries of Africa are subdivided into many tribes of varied sizes, with distinctive characteristics and dialects.

Colonial powers—and to some extent, missionaries—misused the positives of tribalism and emphasized its weaknesses to divide and rule African peoples. Thus today, in some parts of Africa, we see deep problems along the lines of tribalism that were encouraged by colonial powers and some missionaries. By favoring one tribe over another through educating and assigning desirable jobs to their chosen tribes, enmity was created between these ethnic groups that would not normally arise. As a result some African countries have been plunged into a genocidal bloodbath. In our own church we saw Adventists killing Adventists, their hatred based on tribal divisions that outsiders had planted in their minds. The Adventist Church should have been a positive example, but sadly enough, we found ourselves accused of taking sides in some of the terrible killings.

In every country it is evident that missionaries often employed the tool of tribalism to prolong and strengthen their presence in Africa. The attitude of some missionaries certainly has been, "These people cannot lead each other," meaning a person from one tribe could not be accepted to lead persons from another tribe simply because of his or her ethnic background.

People working in Africa should take advantage of the strong dynamics of what tribes can offer in accomplishing the mission of the church. Often it is possible to introduce an entire tribe to the power of the gospel.

2. Appreciate extended families. In much of Africa the extended family is the basic social unit, and the family is usually linked to a larger society through lineage and clan membership. These "kinship groups" generally tend to exclude marriage among their members, requiring that they marry outside the group.

The "village" is frequently constituted of a single kinship group united by elders of either male or female descent. The extended family is therefore so important and solidifying that individuals should identify themselves with it.

Workers in Africa should seek to strengthen the ties of extended families, inasmuch as they have proved to be a successful tool in nurturing church members. Extended families can offer a strong base for evangelism and follow-up. The church should develop programs to strengthen the positive forces that exist in extended families. Aunts and uncles, for example, play a very important role in cementing families. Consequently, in African society, conversion is not simply the transformation of individuals, but of the family or extended family. Leaders should recognize this positive dynamic in African culture.

3. Respect elderly people. Advanced age is very important in Africa and is equivalent to wisdom. Older people are held in high regard by everyone. Their advice is valued and respected; their leadership is followed. And the older a person becomes, the more revered he or she becomes.

Anyone entrusted with leadership among African peoples must learn to respect and revere elders. Even if they are not educated, age gives elders an edge over younger, more educated workers. Addressing an elderly person by his or her first name is unacceptable and very offensive in Africa; they should be addressed formally, using their surnames. Elderly people are given top priority in every social activity.

4. Extend greetings. Africans, in general, love to greet one another, often engaging in an extended period of such conversation. This behavior is a mark of caring and love for one another, and rises from the concept of the extended family.

When you meet a person for the first time, take a few minutes to extend greetings. Do not rush a greeting, as this will be seen as rude and uncaring. Africans love to socialize, and greeting is a part of it. Learn the appropriate greetings and gestures for the people you are serving, including those for (1) different situations of first meeting, (2) close friends, (3) older folks, (4) persons of the opposite sex, (5) children, and (6) leaders of the church.

5. Value oral traditions. Africa has a great body of oral tradition that provides useful resources for placing an authentic African stamp on communication and can aid in reconstruction of scenes of traditional life. People with these oral talents become noted storytellers, entertainers, and historians; some memorize the genealogy or family history of everyone in a village going back centuries.

Develop your public speaking ability. Learn to preach or present seminars without reading notes. Use quotations from Africans who have impacted the continent with their lives as part of your oral presentation. You will be appreciated by your audience—Africans love to listen to great orators.

6. *Utilize proverbs and riddles in communication.* The use of proverbs and riddles among African people is very common. An effective speaker will ensure that a proverb or riddle is used in every speech.

Effective speech, and resultant social success, depends on a good command of proverbs. Treasured sayings convey the demonstrated wisdom of the ages and therefore serve as a reliable authority in arguments or discussion.

7. *Value national identity.* Africans have a deep-seated pride in their own nations. They want to be identified by their country of origin (e.g., Nigerian, Kenyan, Senegalese, etc.). Avoid generic references such as "Africans" when you are talking of persons of a particular country or nation.

8. *Practice hospitality.* Hospitality is a tradition among African peoples that runs very deep. Visitors or guests are highly appreciated, and special treatment is extended to them. In fact, Africans will do things for their visitors without first asking if this service is desired. They would see such a request as being impolite. Thus, one should never ask a guest or visitor in your home if they are hungry—they will always say no, even when they are starving. Just prepare and serve the food.

9. *Respect social sensitivity regarding sexual issues.* This is what we call a highly sensitive matter, a taboo. Actions related to sexual relations are very private—one does not hug and kiss a spouse, girlfriend, or boyfriend in public, and a daughter or son certainly would not kiss someone in front of his or her parents. Such behavior is viewed as rude and inappropriate.

Respect the idea that anything having to do with sexual relations is a very private matter in Africa. When using Western family life materials, ensure that they are adapted to the African culture before you offend your audience. People will not tell you of the uneasiness they experience while listening to your lectures on sexual life. Because it is a taboo, they will just keep quiet! They won't even respond to your questions or make any comment. You do not discuss taboo matters in public.

10. *Respect education.* Education is a mark of social prestige indicating that "you have arrived." There is great respect for persons who have acquired a higher degree or better education than the societal average. Thus it is expected that respect will be given to people who are highly educated.

11. Support families during death. In most African societies death is a community affair. The whole community, church, or village is impacted. Every person supports the bereaved family. An effective leader should be prepared also to support the affected family, emotionally and economically. You should be at the house, church, and funeral with your whole family, if married. Be prepared to spend many hours in giving consolation to the bereaved.

12. Attend weddings. Weddings are a public affair. The entire community participates, whether one is invited or not. Everyone is expected to be involved. If there is a wedding, do not wait for an invitation. Get involved. Invitations are a new thing in African society and are seen by many as coming from a foreign culture.

13. Understand animistic views of God. In African culture God is seen as a distant, unapproachable Creator, a Supreme Being who reflects His nature in lower spiritual beings. He is viewed as the impersonal power that permeates all of nature.

A successful leader should study this view carefully and meet African people at this point as you talk to them about the God of the Bible. Take them from the known (animistic teachings) to the unknown (biblical teachings). The spiritual transition will be fruitful. How I wish our early church pioneers had followed this simple approach instead of condemning the way Africans worshiped and calling such worship paganism. Africans, in general, are very religious, and this could be credited to their belief in animistic teachings. There is something special about the deep spirituality that develops when an African becomes a Christian; it is quite engaging and contagious. Africans have the ability, through their naturalness, to impact the world for good.

14. Tell stories. Africans love stories. In the villages, elderly people will sit around fires in the evening telling stories to young people. Even in the cities, older people have the habit of relating stories to the younger generations. Storytelling is a tool among Africans, used to pass on moral teachings in the family or community. Storytelling is an effective tool that may be included in your preaching, teaching, or seminar presentations.

15. Share music. Africans are a happy people; they sing with joy, and they express this joy by way of emotional dance movements. In African dance, there is no physical touching. African dance is either mimetic or spontaneous. By mimetic, it replicates or reenacts some important event (e.g., the harvest) or historical occurrence. Spontaneous dance is the exhilarating physical expression that accompanies joyous occasions.

A person working in Africa should learn to appreciate the way the Africans sing and express their joy in worship rather than condemning their physical expressions of joy. After all, such physical expressions are encouraged in Scripture (Ps. 150).

16. The more you are blessed, the more you give. Africans love to share. When one is blessed with more than others, he/she is expected to share the blessing with those who have less. If you have a car, expect to be asked to assist—to give rides to those who have none. If you pass people on the way while driving, be ready to give a ride.

17. Respect African conceptions of time—"near versus far"/"soon versus distant." Africans want to see it before they get excited. *Today* is more important to them than *tomorrow.* Remember, the people you serve are excited by programs and events that are happening "soon," that are "near." When you make promotions, you will see a slow build-up. Then as you approach the event, more people will be excited with what you are promoting. "Today" is seen as more important than "tomorrow." Thus someone working among African people must be aware of this kind of thinking and not push people too much or blame them for not eagerly supporting the program before it materializes.

Plan your promotions accordingly, and they will work. One may be overwhelmed with the excitement from the people as the deadline draws near.

18. Be restrained in communication. Certain topics of conversation, taboos, areas of conflict resolution, eye contact, gesturing, and physical language should be avoided if inappropriate. In every country these matters should be observed accordingly. A missionary's desire to be frank and to openly express his/her opinions may seem arrogant to Africans.

19. Remember, the community supercedes the individual. Always remember—the community, the *ubuntu,* "us together," is important, as opposed to the individualism of the West. Sometimes leaders believe that Africans are just interested in monetary aid, but far from it. Africans desire community development and training.

The sense of community, which all Africans share, is a binding force despite linguistic and cultural differences. Africans desire to be a blessing to their nation and to their community.

20. Understand leadership and colonialism. It is important to note that the Seventh-day Adventist Church struggled to bring unification in the South African church after independence. Previously, the church supported the apartheid government/institutions by dividing into four separate lists: Whites, Colored, Blacks, and Indians. Unification has been one of those painful exercises in Africa.

Leaders should learn not to be guided by existing governmental pressures, but be proactive when dealing with such problems. When the church fails to do things in a timely and godly manner, such sentiments as suspicion arise within and without the Seventh-day Adventist churches. This approach has cost the church credibility on the continent. People say, "Look at you. If the church is supposed to be an agent of change and you are in a mess, how can you tell us what to do?" The church has the potential—if not the duty—of playing a major role.

21. People are more important than tasks. In general, the peoples of Africa are "people-centered." For Africans, personal feelings are more important than practical things. Westerners sometimes appear to Africans to ride roughshod over other people's feelings for the sake of getting the job done. But for Africans, doing business involves preserving and caring for relationships.

Put people first in your work. Respect their personal feelings. When you are explaining your ideas, learn to be more sensitive in your way of expression, being aware of how your words will affect your friend's feelings. If you have to disagree, express your respect for him or her and speak gently.

22. Respect the people's cultures. Many times leaders seem to be "proud of their cultures and lifestyles." The leader's body language, his or her relaxed way of sitting and rapid way of walking, often seem assertive and prideful to African people. Watch how others sit when they are in conversation. Respect people and their culture for their differences. It is a very easy trap to start thinking one is superior because he or she is from a certain country, and to ridicule their culture because it is different than yours.

Never talk down to people and speak critically of their culture. It is hard to show love when a leader thinks himself or herself superior. It is even harder to build friendships and truly enjoy the association with African people. Keep an open mind and a tolerant heart, and the people and the Lord will love you for it.

Conclusion

Information in this short chapter is offered in hopes of assisting a leader planning to work with Africans. These guidelines will, if followed, make your relationships with the people you serve more effective and satisfying.

For further reading:

Encarta Encyclopedia 98. Microsoft.

Haley, Alex. *Roots: The Saga of an American Family* (1976).

Holper, Thom. *A World of Difference: Following Christ Beyond Your Cultural Walls.* Downers Grove, Ill.: InterVarsity Press, 1981.

Oosterwal, Gottfried, et al. *Servants for Christ.* Berrien Springs, Mich.: Andrews University Press, 1980.

Seamands, John T. *Tell It Well: Communicating the Gospel Across Cultures.* Kansas City, Mo.: Beacon Hill Press, 1982.

Chapter 5

LEADERSHIP INSIGHTS FOR HISPANICS IN THE TWENTY-FIRST CENTURY

By Humberto M. Rasi, Ph.D.

*Director, Education Department,
General Conference of Seventh-day Adventists*

Let's begin with a virtual illustration. Draw on your mental world map a triangle with corners resting on Spain and Mexico in the north and on Argentina in the south. That virtual triangle encompasses 20 Spanish-speaking countries[1] with a population of more than 360 million.[2] Taking into account normal demographic growth in the region, and adding 20 million Spanish-speaking Hispanics residing in the United States, we can estimate that at the beginning of the twenty-first century the total number of Hispanics will have reached the 400 million mark. This figure makes Spanish the third most spoken international language, after Chinese/Mandarin and English.

From a religious perspective, most Hispanics share a general Christian worldview, with a predominance of Roman Catholics and a small but expanding Evangelical-Pentecostal minority. Spanish-speaking Seventh-day Adventists number 2 million and are growing at an average rate of 7 percent per year. This means that Hispanic Adventists constitute about 20 percent of the Adventist world membership.

At this point it is fair to ask: On what basis can Hispanics be considered a distinct group of the world's population? Given the varied ethnic composition, economies, and other differences among Hispanic countries, is it possible to identify any shared cultural features beyond language? And what kind of Christian leader is expected among Hispanics at the start of the new century? This chapter will address those questions.

Land, People, and Language

In 1492, under contract with Queen Isabella of Castile and King Ferdinand of Aragon, Christopher Columbus landed on a small Caribbean island. He and his motley crew, and the many who followed in their wake, brought the Hispanic language and culture to the New World. After a seven-centuries-long occupation of the Iberian Peninsula by the Moors of Northern Africa, Castile and Aragon had emerged as two small but vigorous European kingdoms. As the combined kingdom of Castile and Aragon grew in power, so did the language spoken by its rulers and peoples. Based mainly on Latin, Castilian had been enriched by Arabic words adopted by the common folk and Greek technical expressions borrowed by scholars.

Within a few decades after Columbus's landfall, the conquistadors crisscrossed the Americas, overcoming the three major indigenous empires—the Aztecs, the Mayas, and the Incas—as well as many smaller tribal groups. Settlers followed, bringing tools, seeds, and animals, and began exploiting the newly conquered lands, planting and mining mostly with the forced labor of Indians and, soon after, of African slaves.

The prestige and riches resulting from being the first to discover, explore, govern, and exploit the American colonies greatly enhanced the standing of the kingdom of Castile. It soon dominated the peninsula and, as the kingdom of Spain, became a world power. At the same time, Castilian Spanish became the national language of the empire, including the expanding colonies of the New World. Roman Catholic Christianity, of which Spain was a staunch defender, was carried by missionaries to the farthest reaches of the empire—from California to the Philippines to Patagonia.

Understanding Hispanics

Several collective names have been proposed to identify the Spanish-speaking peoples of the world, each of them having its own limitations. However, when given a choice, most Spanish speakers choose to identify with their country of origin. The term *Hispanic,* which seems the most acceptable, dates back to the second century before Christ, when, in 204 B.C., the Iberian Peninsula was conquered by the Roman general Scipio Africanus. At that time, Rome identified the native inhabitants as "Hispanics," hence the name of the country, Hispania-España (Spain).

During the past 50 years, profound changes have occurred in Hispanic societies, particularly in the Americas. These include the move from regionalism to national consciousness, from agriculture to industrialization, from rural to urban life, and from cultural isolation to globalized communication, all accompanied by the emergence of a middle class in most countries. Because these rapid changes vary in scope among individuals, regions, and countries, it is important to note that the following descriptions and comments are generalizations. People from other cultures wishing to interact successfully with Hispanics would benefit by understanding five important facts:[3]

Leadership Keys

1. Hispanics are united by linguistic and cultural factors, not by race. Hispanics constitute a racial mosaic. They were initially European Caucasians living in the Iberian Peninsula, at times intermarrying with Arabs and other European and Mediterranean peoples. After Columbus's arrival in the New World, Spaniards mixed with indigenous peoples of the Americas, later with transplanted Africans, and, in the recent past, with newer waves of European and Asiatic immigrants. The assimilation of people groups that occurred through the centuries has led Hispanics to be more accepting toward race and color matters than other peoples.

Mexican essayist José Vasconcelos, reflecting on the multiple ethnic backgrounds of the peoples that now populate Hispanic America—indigenous, European, African, and Asiatic—called them "la raza cósmica [the cosmic race]."[4] It is not easy to tell Hispanics apart from other ethnic groups by their physical characteristics, since they represent all skin tones and features combinations—a veritable human rainbow. Most Hispanics define each other in terms of class—the status one occupies in society as a result of education, position, or economic achievement.

The Spanish language is the major unifying factor among Hispanics, with growing print, oral, visual, and electronic media enhancing communication across national boundaries. Native speakers, however, can easily distinguish the differences in pronunciation and vocabulary that characterize the regional use of the Spanish language much as speakers of English can distinguish a speaker of Australian English from a speaker of American or Jamaican English.

In addition to language, Hispanics share a common view of the world that can be outlined as a series of dynamic tensions. They experience life as both joyous and sad—celebrating both *fiestas* and funerals. They express their emotions freely, and at times passionately, reflecting marked swings between passive contemplation and active risk-taking, between dreamy idealism and earthy realism. Personally and collectively, Hispanics also live in tension between individualism and authoritarianism. This trait is reflected in the dictatorships and revolutions that have characterized the political history of most Hispanic countries as they move toward more stable democracies.

2. Hispanics tend to be religious, leaning toward a generalized Christianity that at times assimilates magic and spiritualism. The Christian religion that Spanish missionaries and settlers brought to the New World collided with the various religious practices of the Amerindians. Most of these religions were obliterated, while a few went underground, emerging later as Christo-paganism.

For centuries Roman Catholicism held sway over Hispanics, frequently in alliance with the government and the upperclass. This dogmatic, ritualistic, and clerical Christianity—centered on external ceremonies—caused reactions that ranged from indifference to open antireligiosity. In recent decades reform movements within Hispanic Catholicism have taken the side of the oppressed (liberation theology), promoted the distribution and study of the Bible, and sought to involve the believers in church life.

Two significant recent religious developments among Hispanics have been the emergence of Pentecostal-Charismatic movements and the resurgence of various forms of spiritualism. Concurrently, the number of Hispanic Seventh-day Adventist believers grows steadily, moving on a broad front through personal and public evangelism, education, publications and other media, health-related approaches, as well as social development.

As Hispanic societies move from traditional to modern ways of thinking, people are offered a wider choice of religious options, ranging from nominal Christianity or secularism to Pentecostalism, Bible-based Christianity, and quasispiritualistic practices. At the beginning of the new century, however, the search for spiritual certainty and inner peace continues among millions of Hispanics, with openness toward authentic Christian belief and practice.

3. Hispanics place a high value on the family and on personal relationships, with a strong sense of honor. Interpersonal relationships are of paramount importance for Hispanics, centering in the nuclear family and extending to include relatives and also friends. In traditional Hispanic areas, the home is seen as an almost sacred place. There the father rules as *paterfamilias,* expecting obedience from children and faithfulness from his wife, even if he himself is not always faithful. The mother is usually the family's emotional center and the influential intermediary between the children and the father. The godfather and godmother, in turn, assume some responsibility for the education and financial support of the new child.

These strong kinship ties lead to a heightened sense of personal dignity and family honor. Hispanics are quite sensitive to criticism and react strongly against real or perceived threats to reputation, position, or prestige. Friendship, on the other hand, demands special favors, even when it requires bending the law. In sum, Hispanics tend to be person-oriented rather than time- or rules-oriented.

Rapid and widespread urbanization, with the dismantling of traditional social structures, has had a negative impact on the Hispanic family, resulting in the breakdown of husband-wife relationships and an increasing number of illegitimate and abandoned children.

4. Hispanics favor clear distinctions between male and female roles in society. As indicated above in the description of the Hispanic family, Spanish-speaking societies tend to be conservative in structure, with defined roles for the father and mother. The father is expected to be the main breadwinner, to handle the discipline of children, and to help select a husband for their daughters. Mothers, even if they hold full-time jobs, play a dominant role in managing the home and providing stability and security for the children.

Dress serves to highlight gender differences, with strong opposition to the mere appearance of homosexuality. *Machismo*—the exaggeration of virility or manliness among Hispanics—leads men to feats of bravery but also to view courtship as sexual conquest and to crimes of passion.

Significantly, however, women continue to make substantial advances in Hispanic societies, not only as professionals in most fields but also in politics. Argentina, Nicaragua, and Panama have had democratically elected female presidents in recent decades.

In popular Hispanic Christianity, God is perceived as the distant and severe Father, and Christ as the passive Son—usually depicted as a defenseless baby or as moribund on the cross. This calls for the virgin Mary to serve as intercessor between the believing children and their stern father.

Biblical Christianity has restored the gospel view of a masculine, living Christ who spent most of His life as a carpenter, who faced His enemies courageously, and who walked toward a cruel death for our salvation. The homes of Evangelical Christians also show a radical difference, with deeper commitment and with mutual love and trust among husbands and wives, parents and children.

5. Hispanics have inherited a rich culture and continue to expand it creatively. Soon after the Spanish settled in the Americas, Spain experienced its "golden age," with an extraordinary flourishing of architecture, art, music, and literature. Cervantes and Velazquez—creators of international stature—produced their works during the late 1500s and early 1600s. It was this rich culture that the Spaniards brought with them to the Americas. As early as 1535, books were being printed in Mexico City, and by 1553 the University of Mexico was offering courses. (By way of comparison, Harvard University was founded in 1636.)

Upon arrival, Spanish settlers encountered several civilizations with well-developed cultures, advanced in agriculture, architecture, astronomy, engineering, literature, natural medicine, and sculpture. In addition, smaller indigenous groups were skilled in all kinds of handcrafts. The aesthetic feel and the fertile creativity resulting from the interaction of European, Amerindian, and Afro-American cultures continues to manifest itself to this day in Hispanic culture.

Intellectually, however, Hispanics tend to rely more on individual intuition and insight than on team research and scientific experimentation. One measure of the breadth and preferences of Hispanic culture is to look at the varied fields in which the 20 Hispanic Nobel Prize winners accomplished their work: one in chemistry, 10 in literature, three in medicine, and six in recognition of their efforts for peace.

Christian Leadership Among Hispanics

In preparation for this essay, the author conducted a survey of Seventh-day Adventist Hispanic leaders to elicit their views on Christian leadership now and in the new century.[5] Seventy completed questionnaires were returned by administrators and supervisors with experience in Spanish-speaking countries, including Hispanic leaders in the United States. Respondents were asked questions in three areas of Christian leadership: qualities, skills, and cultural factors. The results are summarized below.

Qualities of a Christian leader valued by Hispanics. Respondents were asked to select and prioritize the top 10 qualities from among 20 options. The results identified the following qualities of a Christian leader, in order of importance:

1. A friend of God.
2. Committed to the mission's success.
3. Trustworthy, responsible, dependable.
4. Honest, a person of integrity.
5. Attitude of servanthood to others.
6. Teachable, willing to learn.
7. Sensitive to other people's needs.
8. Fair, just.

9. Discerning, wise.
10. Morally upright.

Skills of the Christian leader valued by Hispanics. Respondents were then asked to select and prioritize the top 10 skills from among 20 options. The results identified the following skills of a Christian leader, in order of importance:

1. Maintains focus on priorities.
2. Plans and organizes well.
3. Fosters cooperation and teamwork.
4. Delegates responsibility and seeks accountability.
5. Evaluates everything on the basis of God's principles.
6. Motivates and inspires others.
7. Cultivates positive personal relationships.
8. Is flexible in adjusting to new situations.
9. Understands well his/her role and responsibilities.
10. Identifies and mentors future leaders.

Cultural factors relevant for leaders serving Hispanics. Leaders perform better when they understand and respond with sensitivity to cultural factors. In this section of the questionnaire respondents were asked to mark, within a range, the views of Hispanics with respect to five pairs of significant cultural indicators.[6] Refer to the graph on page 57. The x indicates the location, within the range, where respondents felt that Hispanics as a group were in each of the options.

Conclusion

Rapid urbanization and globalized communications are quickly changing the societies in which Adventist Hispanics live and witness. This new social context urgently calls for informed, transformational Christian leaders, capable of envisioning, enabling, and empowering associates and followers—leaders who will strengthen followers' motivation, understanding, maturity, and sense of self-worth in the common pursuit of transcendent goals.[7]

The diversity among Hispanics can be a positive factor in our global village, facilitating greater understanding and unity among the different nations, ethnicities, and cultures of the world.

Hispanic leaders—enthusiastic, knowledgeable, communicative, and hard-working—are ready to make a substantial contribution, beyond boundaries of language and culture, to the advance of Seventh-day Adventist mission in the new century.[8]

Socioeconomic distance:
In this culture it is considered - - - - - - - - x - In this culture it is considered
normal that there be a small normal that there be a large
distance between rich and poor. distance between rich and poor.

Individualism versus collectivism:
In this culture people prefer - - - - - - - - x - In this culture people prefer
to act as individuals rather to act considering the views of
than as members of a group. the group rather than as individuals.

Masculinity versus femininity:
In this culture traits usually - x - - - - - - - - In this culture traits usually
associated with male roles associated with female roles
are considered important: are considered important:
assertiveness, competition, cooperation, solidarity, service,
triumph of the strongest. care for the weak.

Rules versus flexibility:
In this culture people prefer - x - - - - - - - - In this culture people prefer to act
to act following clear norms freely, without reference to clear
established by tradition. norms established by tradition.

Present versus future:
In this culture people prefer - x - - - - - - - - In this culture people prefer
to enjoy the present without to plan, work, and save in order
being too concerned about to enjoy in the future the fruits of
their efforts. the future.

---

[1] Argentina, Bolivia, Chile, Colombia, Costa Rica, Cuba, the Dominican Republic, Ecuador, El Salvador, Guatemala, Honduras, Mexico, Nicaragua, Panama, Paraguay, Peru, Puerto Rico (a free associate state of the United States), Spain, Uruguay, and Venezuela.

[2] Based on *World Factbook 1998,* produced by the U.S. Central Intelligence Agency and available on the CIA website home page. On the basis of observation, the author of this essay assumes that even those ethnic groups that, while citizens of Spanish-speaking countries, use an indigenous language to communicate among themselves also utilize Spanish to interact with the majority population.

[3] Although somewhat dated, Eugene A. Nida's book, *Understanding Latin Americans* (South Pasadena, Calif.: William Carey Library, 1974), continues to provide valuable insights on this subject.

[4] José Vasconcelos, *La Raza Cósmica* (1925).

[5] The survey, conducted in August 1999, included Adventist leaders (56 male and 14 female) with administrative experience in 17 Hispanic countries, including the United States and Puerto Rico. Twenty-seven of the respondents carry administrative responsibilities at various levels in the Seventh-day Adventist Church organization, and the same number are administrators of Adventist educational institutions. The remaining respondents serve as managers or administrators in other church-related entities—hospitals, pub-

lishing houses, etc. Interested readers may request a full copy of the report in Spanish by e-mailing the author at: *102555.2215@compuserve.com.*

[6] These factors were adapted from Geert Hofstede, "Cultural Constraints in Management Theories," in J. Thomas Wren, ed., *The Leader's Companion* (New York: The Free Press, 1995), pp. 253-270.

[7] See Bernard M. Bass, "Does the Transactional-Transformational Leadership Paradigm Transcend Organizational and National Boundaries?" *American Psychologist* 52, No. 2 (1997): 130-139.

[8] The author wishes to thank Roberto Clouzet, Sylvia Rasi Gregorutti, and Silvia Sicalo for their assistance in the development of this essay.

Chapter 6

LEADERSHIP INSIGHTS FOR EUROPEAN CAUCASIANS IN THE TWENTY-FIRST CENTURY

By Jonathan Gallagher, Ph.D.

Associate Director of News and Information,
General Conference of Seventh-day Adventists

The primary challenge facing leaders of European constituencies is that Europeans don't want to be led! The European preoccupation is with consensus and collegiality. Leaders who wish to be accepted must make sense, provide evidence for their positions and decisions, and communicate effectively so that they are understood.

For while the term *European* embraces many nations, cultures, and thought patterns, there are commonalities and perspectives in Europe that identify a widespread and specific attitude, particularly to leadership.

"Plane" Speaking

I'm sitting in a plane flying into Munich, Germany. Behind me are a couple of businessmen talking, one French, the other English.

"My boss is just so crazy," says the Englishman. "He keeps on telling me what to do. It's just not acceptable. As if he doesn't know better! He should really listen to his workers instead of making unreasonable demands."

"That's nothing," replies the Frenchman. "My boss is far worse. He demands that I do what he says. I told him to try it. He doesn't know how. How foolish!"

There exists a widespread rejection of many managerial techniques, especially if it's perceived that the leader has no knowledge of the job in question. Practical experience and understanding are valued over hierarchy and authority.

Leadership Keys

1. Understand the role of autonomy and individualism in Europe. Modern European society affirms the twin concepts of personal autonomy and individualism. While this does support a strong belief in personal responsibility—you are responsible for your own actions and destiny—on the other hand, this means you do not believe others have any authority to affect your life's direction. The "I'm in charge of my life" syndrome makes it hard for any leader to impact the thoughts and actions of others except by appeal to agreed-upon norms. In other words, individualism militates against leadership since it makes everyone a self-appointed leader of himself or herself. Leaders must tap into mutually agreed concepts that will not violate these "principles" of "I know what is best for me."

However, if it is understood that the leader is supportive of such individualistic rights, then acceptance of leadership can be achieved as a means to self-fulfillment. Those who wish to lead Europeans must focus on elements that bring leaders and their constituencies closer together. No one wants to be known as a follower!

As a result, the most successful leaders often do not identify themselves using conventional leadership terms. They speak of their colleagues, not their employees. The talk about consensus decisions, not the director's dictates. They seek affirmation based, not on their position, but on why others value them.

2. European leadership values are based, not so much on where you are in the organization, but on who you are. Such concepts as "Respect must be earned," "Authority comes with success," and "Actions speak louder than words" point to the valuing process being results-dependent. In other words, while the leader may occupy a certain position associated with power and authority, recognition will come only as the leader achieves what is needed and is considered of value. "Leadership is action, not position," says Donald McGannon.

So the successful leader in Europe will look to build a wide base of support based, not on appeals to structure or discipline, but on basic concepts of truth and right. Directives must make sense, or they will be ignored. Decisions must be credible, or they will be laughed at. Policies must be reasonable, or they will be resisted.

In contemporary Europe there is nothing more damaging to a leader than to be dismissed with humor. A European politician whose attacks were offhandedly dismissed as being "savaged by a dead sheep" found his credibility waning. The media take perverse delight in holding leaders up to ridicule—so much so that leaders are almost expected to be foolish. The successful leader in Europe will try to make sure that his or her leadership style is believable and sensible, not arrogant or pompous.

What Europeans value most of all are leaders with vision, not the authoritarianism of the past. A visionary leader makes the future happen in the present. People want someone to believe in, not someone to obey. In the words of Napoleon: "A leader is a dealer in hope."

European cynicism and skepticism are directed particularly at leaders. The vicar who runs off with the church organist, the chairman who absconds with company funds, the police chief convicted of corruption—these are stories of the day that society feeds on. The scandals of the past and present do much to undermine confidence in leadership.

Today's leaders have to be blameless and honest, without becoming pretentiously pious. Too many good European leaders have been forced from office because of foolish indiscretions that they considered unimportant.

3. Appreciate the role that leader honesty plays in communication. European society is critical, judgmental, hypocritical, and unforgiving when it comes to its leaders. So to lead in Europe, a direct and honest approach is essential. What is valued is integrity and an ability to communicate at the common level. To appear condescending or aloof is fatal—these are the unforgivable sins of the past that are not tolerated in a pluralistic Europe that aims at joint approaches and multiple directions. The eccentric leader giving unquestioned orders from a distant ivory tower has no place in modern Europe.

4. Stress collegiality. The opinions of others are important and should be sought. That does not mean leadership by committee, but making sure that there is input. People recognize that leaders cannot please everyone all the time. But they do demand that they are heard.

In dealing with dissatisfied workers and hostile colleagues, I would arrange a meeting, and often such angry people would shout for a while, but I made it a policy always to listen. After venting their dissatisfaction for a while, it was usually possible to discuss alternatives and possible remedies. On some occasions I would thank them for their time and their opinions, and then make it clear that in this case I could not accommodate their wishes. The frequent comment was "Well, at least you listened," and it was enough.

There are many methods to promote idea-sharing and the sense that individuals have a voice. What people fear is that leaders are not listening to them and that they have no control over their destiny. The concept of consensus, of mutual participation, brings other positive aspects to any organization—such as the sense of joint ownership, direct involvement, and personal interest. People should care about the company they work for, the societies they belong to, the church they attend—for if they don't, then both organization and leader will be seen as optional and replaceable.

5. Provide a clearly understood vision. Stand for something that is valued, and show that you care about it. Leaders need to be seen as concerned with more than management—of making a profit or continuing the status quo.

A British discount jeweler who in an unguarded moment spoke dismissively of his merchandise saw his company collapse. People want their leaders to believe too.

And they want their leaders to have a clear focus of the vision. This needs to become part of the organization's work ethic, a rallying point for values above monetary worth. Leaders who can show where they are going and why will be followed, even though those following may not term themselves followers!

6. Communicate, communicate, communicate! The great mistake is to fail to share the vision, to forget to speak about collegiality, to take the communication process for granted. This is fatal. You cannot lead without sharing your ideas regularly and extensively. Use all the means you have: speaking through video and TV and audio, writing in newsletters and papers and memos, communicating through electronic means in e-mails, Web sites, faxes—whatever. You cannot assume that people understand what you are doing and saying, and if there is doubt, then there is doubt in leadership.

Take the time to formulate thoughts and to make ideas concrete. Make sure there is a regular opportunity to spend time on this. Make appointments to just talk with those whom you would not normally contact. One very useful activity, I found, was just to be present and available on a frequent basis. That resolved many potential problems before they grew big and unmanageable.

7. Don't be afraid to be decisive. As someone once put it, even a wrong decision is better than no decision. Even in jaundiced Europe, leaders are expected to make firm and positive decisions. Sometimes there may be grumbling and second-guessing, but decisions—especially if they are well thought out and explained—will be accepted. As the Latin writer Publius Syrus wrote in the first century B.C.: "Anyone can hold the helm when the sea is calm." Leading when it's rough is the mark of true leadership.

But in deciding, again, demonstrate that you have listened and considered carefully. The leader who makes an instant decision without thought and care will be seen as a maverick and, consequently, distrusted.

The Roman author Tacitus—a European, if he had but known it—commented that "reason and judgment are the qualities of a leader." Making good judgments, being reasoned and reasonable—if that is clear, Europeans will agree to be led.

8. *Recognize your own limitations.* Europeans will respect a leader who does not claim infallibility and omniscience. In fact, admission of insufficiencies by leaders gives them a paradoxical attractiveness to modern society. A leader is not supposed to be Superman, nor is he expected to be proficient in every area of leadership activity. Wise leaders will recognize this and make sure their deficiencies are made up by others around them, and that they—the others—get the credit for so doing.

Some leaders believe it is an admission of failure to say they are deficient in some way. But European society is far more ready to recognize that no one person can provide every skill and ability than most leaders think. Tolerance has become a widespread motto across Europe, and this even applies to leaders. As long as they do not become self-absorbed and full of ideas of personal aggrandizement, leaders are tolerated. In the European model, leaders are seen almost as a necessary evil, but leaders will continue to be effective as long as they themselves recognize their humanity with all its faults and failings.

9. *See leadership as people development.* Leadership in Europe is welcomed as it seeks to develop the goals and potentials of others. Attempts to stifle these aspirations may succeed for a while if supported by force, but the ultimate result is hostility and rejection, and the collapse of the organizational system. The history of Europe is full of leaders who unwisely sought control through force rather than through cooperation and people development. Perhaps that is why Europeans are so sensitive to any kind of pressured leadership, preferring leaders who, while strong and decisive in their visions and goals, still wish the same for those they lead.

Modern European leaders may not be idealistic, philanthropic benefactors, but they are conscious of the needs of the people in their personal growth. The wish of everyone to achieve ambitions, to make a difference in life, to find meaning and purpose, will be respected by those who claim the same for themselves in positions of leadership.

10. *Concentrate on higher values.* Do not be satisfied with the bottom-line balance sheet or other materialistic measures of success. Leaders are expected to have higher values, to place a stress on trust and confidence and ethical ideals.

Nineteenth-century British prime minister Benjamin Disraeli said it well: "I repeat . . . that all power is a trust; that we are all accountable for its exercise." Leaders are placed in positions of trust, which is why their failings in this area are viewed with such horror. Power is given conditionally, and if that trust is broken, then leaders can expect no mercy. Acting responsibly, doing business with ethical principles, recognizing a higher authority—all this is the measure of a good leader. Despite the cynicism noted before, modern Europeans still aspire to such principles, or at least want their leaders to do so!

This also means that leaders will not only be concerned with their primary responsibilities but also recognize their commitments to other areas of need. Community service, the support of good causes, the identification with those who are in want—as leaders demonstrate their practical involvement in such concerns they will be appreciated the more by those they seek to lead.

Says Walter Lippmann: "Leaders are the custodians of a nation's ideals, of the beliefs it cherishes, of its permanent hopes, of the faith which makes a nation out of a mere aggregation of individuals."

Conclusion

Just in case leaders are inclined to see themselves as permanent fixtures, consider these words of Emperor Napoleon Bonaparte once more: "The throne is but a piece of wood covered with velvet."

That's a humbling perspective, especially from a European leader who at one stage in his career had much of Europe under his control. Of course, his leadership style is not one most Europeans would want to emulate today! But his recognition of the temporal and transient nature of leadership is important to remember. As he reflected back on his achievements from his lonely exile on the island of St. Helena, we can wonder what he saw as his greatest contributions. Leaders, particularly, must reflect on what they want to achieve, and why. It is not enough just to say that it was possible. From a European perspective, leadership must be viewed as a way of benefiting others, of not being primarily concerned with self, and of providing a visionary "future in the present."

The leadership methods of the past will not work. Europe has seen too many absolute monarchs, harsh despots, and self-promoting dictators. The concepts of communal leadership, of representative government, of open discussion, are too deeply ingrained to be ignored by potential leaders.

The five freedoms are identified as:

The freedom to be.

The freedom to do.

The freedom to know.

The freedom to go.

The freedom to believe.

Leaders will try to work through the advancement of these freedoms, recognizing that their success will depend, not on their authority, but on the degree to which others grant them the opportunity to provide leadership. Those seeking to lead European constituencies must understand the societal context and the community's vision for the future that will contain support for those five freedoms as part of any "contract" between leaders and the led.

Chapter 7

LEADERSHIP INSIGHTS FOR NATIVE AMERICANS IN THE TWENTY-FIRST CENTURY

By Robert Burnett, M.A.

Director of Native American Ministry,
North American Division of the Seventh-day Adventist Church

Jesus Loved Others More Than Himself

Native Americans are a very spiritual people. Providing effective leadership for Native American constituencies, however, can be achieved only through love. Having experienced authority, domination, power, punishment, and showmanship, they know what love is and from whom it originates. Thus the key to accomplishing the task of working successfully among the Native peoples of the Americas is allowing God, our Creator and Sustainer, to reveal His love through you to those who accept the urging of His Holy Spirit. Any leader entrusted with the servanthood task of leadership must first and always act within the boundaries of God's transcendent love. This article, in the interest of encouraging this type of leadership, presents a short history of interaction with Native Americans followed by seven important recommendations, not necessarily in prioritized order, for those selected to lead institutions comprised of Native Americans.

Jesus Knew History

The key to understanding Native American culture is to understand their past. This chapter cannot provide all a leader should know before engaging in a long relationship with a Native American constituency. However, to start, the early diary pages that Christopher Columbus wrote after landing on the islands in the Americas describes a happy, contented people who are generous, kind, loving, and without disease, war, or strife.

Sadly, though, as explorer after explorer reached the Americas, the Native inhabitants suffered. Wealth in the form of gold and valuable natural resources attracted the visitors as they discovered new ways to exploit this "land of milk and honey." Within 20 years of Columbus's landing on the island, the peaceful and happy indigenous people living there were virtually wiped out through the introduction of new diseases for which they had no immunity, slavery, and ethnic and religious cleansing.

One could say that the Europeans saw themselves as a new Israel entering a new promised land, instituting ethnic disenfranchisement and enforced assimilation procedures that continue even today. Why would the Creator allow this to happen to a people described in such a way as Columbus described the first people he encountered?

It should be understood that originally South, Central, and North America as we know it did not exist. These lands were inhabited by the people we term Native Americans. Before the "discovery" of the Americas, the indigenous people living in these regions passed information primarily through traveling messengers, and the various cultures shaped and influenced each other from the tip of South America to the North Pole. Slowly these groups began to worship the sun and other things provided in nature by the Creator.

For many Native Americans, the last 500-plus years of slavery induced by European conquerors resulted in a "walking away" from the Creator. However, just as Israel had prophets and prophecies of hope, so God has provided for the Native people of the Americas. Much has been misunderstood and forgotten about the original beliefs of these peoples. Indeed, even most tribal leaders will quickly acknowledge that many of the supposed "traditional" dances and ceremonies of the people are the result of interactions with non-Native peoples over the past 200 years. What has truly kept the Native cultures alive are the prophecies and the continuing belief that the Creator will return to cleanse the earth and reward the good people.

During this time of suffering, the Native peoples have become "the forgotten peoples." Little is said in the news in North America concerning the poverty and suffering of Native Americans. While much is done for the rest of the world by the richest nation on earth, those living in government-established territories termed "reservations" face conditions of stark poverty. In a land with the most advanced media capabilities, few realize that the unemployment rate on many reservations is close to 90 percent, and that 32 percent of Native families live below the poverty line in the United States. The death rate for Native people is 140 percent higher than the general population, and the teen suicide rate is 60 percent higher than Whites. Some 80 percent of Native Americans experience an unexpected sudden or violent death, and the life span of the typical Native American male is 46 years, compared to 72 years for a White American male. Government officials report housing conditions far below the standards for the rest of North America.

While the history of governmental interaction with Native Americans may appear comprehensive at first, scholars confirm that most of what is being taught in the classroom and reported in print is greatly distorted. In the past few years, the truth has resulted in the changing of names on monuments, changing the word "battle" to "massacre" in memorial locations, apologies by governmental and religious leaders, and the acknowledgment by the United States Congress that treaty land funding in excess of hundreds of billions of dollars never reached the Native peoples, but was absorbed by other branches of the government, such as the Department of Agriculture.

In the past 10 years the situation has evolved to a point at which the government now recognizes tribal lands and some Native peoples as sovereign (self-governing). This has resulted in new methods of distributing funds, new funding investments, and a strong desire by Native leaders to lift their people from poverty. Funding for change is becoming more available as tribal leaders take over the operation of hospitals and schools, and start establishing businesses above and beyond the casinos.

At the same time, Native peoples are seeing the signs given in prophecy for the return of the Creator. Prophecies of most Native nations tell of a resurgence in spirituality before the return of the Creator, and many prophecies refer to a "black book." The forgotten peoples have a desire to return to the Creator, but first they need to rediscover their heritage with Him.

Leadership Keys

1. Understand the history of these forgotten peoples before you engage them, just as Jesus knew the history of His people before He taught them. You must especially come to understand and become sensitive to the history, culture, and needs of the particular community with which you are going to work.

2. Be thoroughly familiar with your Bible. Nothing is more important in Native cultures than "walking in your words." Knowing the Bible and living the Bible go together in Native leadership. Jesus answered by saying, "It is written . . ." Now, does this mean they expect me to be perfect? The Bible does not say any human being is perfect; rather that we have all strayed. What it does say is that God's people are a people of

68

love, and that they strive to do His will in all things. So what are your motives? If you know your Bible and walk in its words, the motives for your actions will mirror the principles you teach from the Bible. You will find that Native people want to see you succeed. They will look for your consistency in walking this new path, and if you do it, you will find that they will be pleased to follow.

A priority in preparation for leadership of Native American constituencies is Bible study. To "walk in your words," you need to know the words of the Bible. As you follow this principle, you will enjoy your experience with the Native American peoples. You will find that others will have a great desire to join you after they have seen your walk.

3. *Know your life and leadership purpose.* Before speaking, let alone leading, shouldn't we know why we are here and what we have been sent to do? Some Native Adventists may advocate that you join certain movements to show true leadership. But remember, the Native American peoples may be poor as people groups, but they are extremely sharp when it comes to spiritual matters. If you come as a spiritual person, understand that what has come before you in the same cloak has at times been genocide. Be prepared to communicate in their terms what vision you have been given that brings you to them.

Jesus knew why He came into this world and for what reason the breath of the living God passed through His lungs. He knew He had not been sent to overthrow the Roman leaders. Within the Native cultures, a person is sent out to receive a vision of their future, the reason they exist. A principle is that nothing is to live unto itself. So why do you exist? What is your vision? Who sent you? Did you come here because you didn't make it at another church, institution, or hospital? Maybe you wanted a mission field and this is all they had to offer? Have you been chosen to bring to the people a message or guide them to a new future? Why are you here?

4. *Choose service over dominance when leading.* Leadership has a different meaning to different groups of people. To some, a leader is a figurehead. To others, a leader is a pusher of ideas to generate action. To Native American peoples, a leader is respected, proven to walk in his or her own words, and known by the aura of success provided by a force greater than himself or herself.

Throughout their history, American Indians have had great leaders who, through visions from above, rose to be great men and women when they submitted themselves to be followers/servants of their Creator.

Great Native American leaders have always lived a life of self-denial, putting others before themselves. The speech and actions of such leaders have always been with respect to what is best for the people, not what is good for themselves. Do not confuse leaders of some nations today for the great leaders in Native history, any more than you would confuse some leaders in America today for the great leaders in American history.

As Christians, we believe all authority comes from God. Being a leader to Native Americans cannot happen until you have been blessed by God with an unselfish heart, a servant attitude, a humble spirit, and a real faith that the one Creator-God is in control of all things.

5. Understand Native Americans' learning preferences. Native Americans are a tribal people, and most of their societies are matriarchal in nature. Elders are held in great esteem for their knowledge, experience, and wisdom. Parenting is somewhat loose, but Native Americans love and value their children highly.

The culture is verbal, so most good instruction is both verbal and experiential. Native peoples are visual and audio learners. Studies have shown that most Native peoples are "right-brain" learners and have a "melancholy" temperament. A leader would find Native people very spiritual and artistic, but many with somewhat low self-esteem—largely because of their past history and poor economic conditions.

The typical Native person is proud, shy, and straightforward when speaking. Native people are naturally very trusting and accept words as promises quicker than most, which explains why they tend to be somewhat sensitive because of the past history of broken promises. Loyalty is easily established and can be very strong, but broken promises are not easily forgotten.

A leader planning to enter Native ministry would do well to study the exchange between Jesus and the woman at the well, and stories of Jesus' encounters with the Gentiles in 2 Corinthians 4 and Colossians 2, 3.

6. Respect Native Americans' approaches to time. Many Native Americans, the Navajo especially, believe that rushing about on a schedule is stressful and therefore wrong. Things are to come about in the Creator's good time, without stress. This being the case, unless the importance of worship as a family is understood, many Native people will arrive late at church or an appointment—"whenever they get there." Pushing or prodding for greater punctuality will only create stress, which is viewed as something evil created to shorten lifespans, create division, prevent rest, and cause other feelings that are out of touch with goodness.

7. Empathize with the poverty and suffering of Native peoples.
Jesus focused on the Father who sent Him, and Native people prefer dealing with the "short version" of the gospel as well. As mentioned earlier, to the Native mind, a person will reveal in action his or her focus in life, business, and priorities. As a leader, the time you spend with your Creator, Sustainer, Father, and Saviour will be reflected in your relations to others, priority of prayer time, and fairness of decisions. This will reveal your motives and purpose for coming among the people.

Having read everything in this chapter thus far, you may question why Native Americans are in poverty in spite of their proud attitudes and focused perspectives. A question can also be asked concerning spiritual sensitivity versus the high levels of drinking, drugs, domestic violence, and the lack of parenting. A fair leader who studies the culture will find that any people group that has lost a portion of their identity and culture will fall into economic disarray. After such a long time in poor economic conditions, the people lose hope.

Native society has been demeaned for hundreds of years. Even our own churches use the Native names of people groups in place of animal names for mascots or Pathfinder trophies. Native men were hunters and gatherers, but the right to do both has been denied. Discrimination near Native centers is very high.

Conclusion

My wife is Swiss. She can return to Switzerland at any time to see her rightful culture. Other people can go to Africa, Europe, or the Far East for a visit—to see the dances of their culture, to participate in ceremonies, to return home with a piece of their heritage. If Native American peoples leave what little land they have left, they and their children's children will have no language, no heritage, and no traditions to return to. They will cease to exist as a people group. Many Native Americans believe that this has been the design of the government and organized religion in the United States for much of its history.

Jesus saw what people were meant to be rather than what they were when He passed by. He saw the good in people. He renewed their hope and provided the truth of their heritage as humans. He loved them beyond their understanding, before they were clean, vegetarian, or lived healthfully. He inspired faith, taught truth, treated with fairness, and served with compassion. Leaders entering Native ministry will not fully understand the mind-set of the Native peoples unless they walk among them as Jesus walked among us—with a loving heart and the desire to restore what was lost in Eden.

For further reading:

Briner, Bob, and Ray Pritchard. *More Leadership Lessons of Jesus.* Nashville, Tenn.: Broadman and Holman Publishers, 1998.

Champagne, Duane. *Native America: Portrait of the Peoples.* Washington, D.C.: Visible Ink Press, 1994.

Crow Dog, Mary. *Lakota Woman.* New York: Harper Perennial, 1990.

Parker, Arthur C. *Parker on the Iroquois.* Syracuse, N.Y.: Syracuse University Press, 1968.

Peterson, Scott. *Native American Prophecies.* New York: Paragon House, 1990.

Utter, Jack. *American Indians: Answers to Today's Questions.* Lake Ann, Mich.: National Woodlands Pub. Co., 1993.

Videotapes:

Ancient America Series: More Than Bows and Arrows, by Regional Corp./Camera One, 1992.

How the West Was Lost I and II (seven videos), by Filmic Archives, 1993.

Chapter 8

LEADERSHIP INSIGHTS FOR AFRICAN-AMERICANS IN THE TWENTY-FIRST CENTURY

By C. Garland Dulan, Ph.D.

*Associate Director of Education,
General Conference of Seventh-day Adventists*

One can approach the study of leadership through a search of the literature in such subject areas as organizational management, organizational sociology, educational leadership, and psychology. There is a plethora of characteristics associated with effective leadership across these subject areas.

Jay A. Conger suggests that "simply possessing certain traits associated with leadership is no guarantee that one will emerge a leader. . . . One must be motivated to lead." [1]

Although leadership traits and motivation are necessary, they are not sufficient guarantors of effective leadership. Effective leaders must also possess an awareness and sensitivity to the needs and values of others. This is where diversity and leadership intersect. Max DePree, chairman of Herman Miller, Inc., the primary innovator in the United States furniture industry for 60 years, suggests that leadership is an art, something to be learned over time, not simply acquired by reading books. He indicates that effective leaders recognize and endorse the diversity of people's gifts, talents, and skills.[2] Historically, this perspective has been central to leadership in the African-American church and community.

This chapter focuses on the art of leadership among African-Americans. The information presented reflects a review of the literature on leadership, my personal experiences over a period of approximately 20 years of work with African-Americans, and recent interviews with African-Americans who are currently in leadership positions within the Seventh-day Adventist Church. In this chapter I examine: (1) the context of leadership, (2) characteristics of groups, and (3) characteristics and methods of effective leaders.

The Leadership Context

"Leadership context" refers to the organizational framework in which tasks are conceived, understood, and performed. For example, Sondra Thiederman suggests that supervisors familiarize themselves with the culture of the ethnic groups with which they are working, including being informed about their value system, expectations, and desires.[3] Doing so increases leadership effectiveness and decreases job stress for both the employee and the supervisor.

While some general principles of leadership apply regardless of context, they can be applied most effectively by taking context into account. For example, in health care, finance, and in business relations, persons in leadership positions are often advantaged by having a more complete knowledge of facts than those seeking their assistance. Even though an individual may have a general knowledge of health, when visiting a health-care professional's office, one is usually seeking help, is willing to pay for it, and is thus more amenable to following "professional" or specialized advice.

This is only partly the case in educational and religious contexts. In settings in which mature students enroll in school and select classes, and when church members serve in congregations or on church boards, they not only interact with leadership in a largely voluntary setting but also may feel they have to make their own decisions regardless of what an adviser or leader proposes.

Leadership in the Black community has, in large part, emerged from and been nurtured by the Black church. According to C. Eric Lincoln and Lawrence H. Mamiya: "Not only did it [the Black church] give birth to new institutions such as schools, banks, insurance companies, and low income housing; it also provided an academy and an arena for political activities, and it nurtured young talent for musical, dramatic, and artistic development."[4]

Organizational forms of the African-American church generally favored charismatic (appeal of personality and preaching style) to bureaucratic-type leadership (records and typical organizational forms). Even today among African-American Seventh-day Adventist churches, recognized leaders are expected to possess proper educational credentials and, in addition, to have charismatic appeal. We must consider this aspect of the African-American culture when discussing leadership within the church.

Context has much to do with a perception of what leadership approaches are deemed acceptable. Manfred F. R. Kets de Vries suggests that leadership is the exercise of power, and the quality of leadership—good, ineffective, or destructive—depends on an individual's ability to exercise power.[5] The power approach probably works well in crisis situations such as in war or police and medical emergencies in which key individuals are given wide ranges of authority because of the critical nature of the situation. However, in church and educational settings, leaders usually do not have ultimate authority, and may even be considered colleagues of those in the congregation or institution.

According to Conger: "The leadership role can be conferred by followers, but they cannot be forced to grant it."[6] A church pastor, for example, does not have the power to command a congregation to perform an act, because members both elect to join a congregation and often elect or help select the pastor. Autocratic leadership, such as attempting to force a pastor's ideas on a congregation, simply will not work. Rather, persuasion may be the better approach. Leaders must be aware of what methods are most effective in the context in which they are working.

Leadership Keys

1. Consider the multicultural composition of the Black community. An important issue of context is the multicultural environment in which African-American churches, conferences, and schools operate. Often, from the perspective of external viewers, groups composed of persons of color are seen as one culture, rather than what in reality are multicultural groups. In these multicultural settings, the challenge for leadership, according to Gilbert W. Fairholm, is to deal with the fact that the many cultures represented include values, ideals, or behaviors that work against effective, coordinated performance.[7] (For example: African-Americans and Afro-Caribbeans may view "mainstreaming" in different ways.) Further, Fairholm argues that the leader's job is to create other values that supersede inappropriate ones introduced into the organization by diverse people and assist in replacing them with those of a common direction and commitment around which many people can gather to accomplish socially useful results.[8]

A critical task for an African-American leader, then, is to understand the social context in which he or she is operating. An understanding of context enhances a leader's ability to influence others toward a view beyond which they may presently see, and aids in guiding them to an agreed-upon destination. Initially Christ had difficulty leading His disciples because they did not understand the context of His mission. By assisting His disciples in understanding His context of work, Christ was able to influence their understanding of the common goal toward which they could work together. Once the disciples understood, they spread the gospel to the then-known world.

2. Consider the group's characteristics. Understanding characteristics of the group can enhance the leader's ability to empower the team to reach goals, coach them to increase effectiveness, and mentor members to increase responsibility. It is important that a leader become aware of the group's strengths and of the members' levels of expertise, openness to change, and frame of reference.

In voluntary organizations in which members are well informed, a leader would be wise to seek advice, especially from key individuals within the group. A leader must be willing to explore ways to identify the key individuals. He or she also needs to be open and listen in order to determine what the needs are of those to be led.[9] Solomon's wisdom is instructive: "Follow good counsel and you will succeed" (Prov. 20:18, Clear Word). While a leader should present a clear vision for the organization or for the task at hand, he or she also needs to be aware of the eagerness for change within the group. Sometimes a leader encounters opposition to ideas presented that may result from a general unwillingness on the part of the group to accept change.

It is important to know one's constituency, whether elected or appointed to office. Professionals expect to hear several viewpoints presented; they will generally resist being led to a leader's own conclusions unless they have reviewed the facts themselves and have arrived at similar conclusions on their own. New leaders should be aware that sometimes resistance from a group is related to the past mistakes of a previous leader or to the extraordinarily positive relationships the group may have developed with a previous leader whom they were not ready to release.

When a leader undertakes to persuade a congregation, conference constituency, faculty, or administrative staff to embark on a campaign to raise money for a building, church, or office complex, it is imperative to know the group's frame of reference. Is it long-term or short-term? It is common to find African-Americans in the church who hold to the concept that since Jesus Christ is coming soon, one need not pay too much attention to long-term projects. The words of the song "Don't Take Time to Pay No Mind, Cause I Ain't Got Long to Stay" conveys their thoughts.

In a democratic environment, the expected approach to problem-solving usually involves committees. While committees are useful, they have limited utility when decisions must be carried out. A leader must understand that he or she cannot hold a committee accountable; individuals must be held accountable. To implement decisions requires real, live persons who are willing to accept the responsibilities of leadership.

3. *Consider the methods of effective leaders.* "The measure of leadership," according to Max DePree, "is not the quality of the head, but the tone of the body. . . . Are the followers reaching their potential? Are they learning? Serving?"[10] Effectiveness must be understood as enabling others to reach their potential—both their personal potential and their corporate or institutional potential. A way to improve effectiveness is to encourage roving leadership, leadership that arises and expresses itself at varying times and in varying situations, according to the dictates of those situations. Roving leaders lead in special situations.[11]

While the literature is replete with information regarding the characteristics and methods of effective leaders, it does not speak directly to which methods work best with African-Americans. From a series of conversations over the past two decades, and from a series of recent open-ended interviews with several Black leaders, each of whom had more than 20 years of experience in leadership positions, I gained insights into what they considered to be the most important characteristics of a leader and the most effective methods of leading African-Americans. These leaders served in a variety of settings that included health care, churches, government, administration, education, and business/finance. This section provides a summary of information gained from those interviews and informal conversations.

I asked a series of 10 questions to African-American leaders and members, among which were the following:

1. What do you consider to be the three most important personal qualities of a leader?

2. What methods have you found to be most effective in leading African-Americans?

3. What was/is your greatest challenge in attempting to lead African-Americans?

4. What have you found to be some of the most important considerations that must be cared for prior to attempting to lead African-Americans?

5. If you wanted to give advice to a younger person who aspired to become a leader of African-American people, what word(s) of advice would you share with them? What to do? Or what not to do?

Following are some characteristics these leaders felt were most important:

Table 1
Characteristics of an Effective African-American Leader

1. Honesty.
2. Respects the opinions of others. Is open to receiving advice from others.
3. Ability to be decisive.
4. Works within the framework of policy.
5. Leads by example and through personal sacrifice.
6. Models leadership skills in business and at home.
7. Shares authority.
8. Is open to criticism.
9. Approaches problem-solving from a holistic perspective.
10. Uses a hands-off management style.
11. Has genuine semipersonal relationships.
12. Has a vision of what can be. Has the ability to implement his or her vision.
13. Has the ability to motivate people to action.
14. Has good communication skills. Knows how to deal with people.
15. Has the ability to socialize and feel comfortable with other Blacks.
16. Uses a biblical mandate in one's approach to leadership.
17. Invites the group most affected by the consequences of a decision to be involved in the decision-making process whenever possible.
18. Is trained well in leadership approaches and is prepared to deal with the consequences of what he or she asks of others.
19. Is an effective Christian and sees things from a Christian perspective.

The above statements show that the respondents felt that personal integrity, modeling, openness, visioning, the ability to communicate well, and Christian commitment were essential qualities for an African-American leader to possess. Additionally, the history of African-Americans demonstrates that effective leaders share the following characteristics:

1. They are committed to a cause.
2. They empower their team or constituency to reach common goals.
3. They seek help with difficult tasks.
4. They coach others to increase their effectiveness.
5. They mentor others to increase their sense of understanding and responsibility.

Effective African-American leaders also serve their people. As one African-American leader put it: "Leaders need to be knowledgeable, trustworthy, and people-centered. They should not be self-centered. They should share credit and allow others to share the spotlight. They should be accessible and available."

"Leaders owe the organization a new reference point for what caring, purposeful, committed people can be in the institutional setting."[12] A leader should attempt to create an environment of trust, allowing for full discussion when necessary, even though the discussion may sometimes seem trivial or unrelated to the point. It is better to bring the group along with you rather than assuming that your knowledge of what is best for them will eventually be understood. This slower, even painful, process may prove to be more effective in the long run.

"A leader must assess capability. A leader must be a judge of people. For leaders choose a person, not a position."[13] Leaders make mistakes. When they do, it is essential that they give an apology. The extent of forgiveness depends often on the extent to which a constituency feels the apology is genuine.

The leader of the future, according to Stephen Covey (1996), must activate several functions, among which is the ability to empower others.[14] "Empowering" refers to how a leader commissions talent, ingenuity, intelligence, and creativity that may be lying dormant within the people of the organization. Empowerment leads toward an ignition of a fire within people that unleashes their latent talents and ingenuity to do whatever is necessary and consistent with the principles agreed upon to accomplish the goals of the organization. Leaders owe people space—freedom in the sense of enabling their gifts to be exercised. They need to give others space so that they may both grow to be themselves and exercise their diversity.[15] This, in essence, is tapping into the abilities and talents of those within the organization.

Table 2 (see page 80) indicates which methods were deemed most effective in leading African-Americans. Note that most of these methods relate to church environments, although many could be used regardless of setting.

Leaders must understand that there is a window of opportunity for leadership within an organization. One can be effective for only so long, not forever. Leaders need to be sensitive enough to pick up cues as to when the window is closing so they will be prepared to exit when change is warranted. To stay longer than is required to do the job or is desired by the organization puts one at considerable emotional risk.

Finally, DePree sums up the progress of an artful leader by saying that "the first responsibility of a leader is to define reality. The last is to say thank you. In between the two, the leader must become a servant and a debtor."[16]

Table 2
Most Effective Methods of Leading African-Americans

1. Have a planned agenda.
2. Be cooperative, not dictatorial.
3. Make use of the various abilities of people in the congregation or group so that success is seen as theirs and yours.
4. At every opportunity, give recognition to others.
5. Try to reach each level of personnel within the organization so they feel an important part of the organization.
6. Find out what things are most important to your constituency, what their backgrounds are, and what their resources are, then coordinate your agenda with theirs.
7. Work by touch, by feel, and by prayer.
8. Present several alternative courses of action to a group.
9. Create an environment of trust within the organization.
10. Allow others to reach their potential without making them feel you are trying to outshine them. Concentrate on effectiveness.
11. Understand the symbolic trappings of a culture.
12. Understand the importance of being international in approach when necessary.
13. Get to know people individually.
14. Seek to be a friend without compromising the integrity of your business responsibilities.
15. Know your business and do your business well.
16. Conduct yourself in a manner above repute regardless of what others may do to you.
17. Rely totally on the Lord and no one else.
18. Practice what you preach.
19. Join Black organizations and professional groups. Socialize with Black people.
20. Familiarize yourself with how things work within the organization you will head.

[1] Jay A. Conger, *Learning to Lead* (San Francisco: Jossey-Bass Publishers, 1992), p. 7.

[2] Max DePree, *Leadership Is an Art* (New York: Doubleday, 1989), p. 7.

[3] Sondra Thiederman, *Bridging Cultural Barriers for Corporate Success* (Lexington, Mass.: Lexington Books, 1991), pp. 145-167.

[4] C. Eric Lincoln and Lawrence H. Mamiya, *The Black Church in the African American Experience* (Durham, N.C.: Duke University Press, 1990), p. 8.

[5] Manfred F. R. Kets de Vries, *Leaders, Fools, and Impostors* (San Francisco: Jossey-Bass Publishers, 1993), p. 22.

[6] Conger, p. 17.

[7] Gilbert W. Fairholm, *Leadership and the Culture of Trust* (Westport, Conn.: Praeger Publishers, 1994), pp. 38-49.

[8] *Ibid.*

[9] Conger, p. 17.

[10] DePree, p. 10.

[11] *Ibid.,* pp. 16, 17.

[12] *Ibid.,* p. 12.

[13] *Ibid.,* p. 17.

[14] Stephen R. Covey, "Three Roles of the Leader in the New Paradigm," in F. Hesselbein et al., eds., *The Leader of the Future* (San Francisco: Jossey-Bass Publishers, 1996), pp. 149-159.

[15] DePree, p. 14.

[16] *Ibid.,* p. 9.

Chapter 9

LEADERSHIP INSIGHTS FOR NORTH AMERICAN CAUCASIANS

By Monte Sahlin, M.Div.

*Vice President for Creative Ministries,
Columbia Union Conference*

This may be an unexpected chapter in this volume. It is also a difficult one to know how to label and introduce. What do we call the people who make up the ethnic majority in the general population of America? The United States census and most demographers label them "non-Hispanic Whites." Within the North American Division of the Seventh-day Adventist Church, administrators have come to refer to them as "Anglos."

There are problems with the word "White." In fact, when the terms White and Black are used to label races, their use is essentially racist in construct. It has become clear today that such use of these terms has little basis in reality. Genetics do not transmit something as complex as "race." The specific physical characteristics of an individual may have little to do with the traditional assumptions about the particular ethnic background of his or her ancestors. For example, people are often surprised to know that my great-grandfather immigrated to the U.S. from Sweden because both my father and I are clearly not blonds. (It could be argued that this surprise is in itself a racist response.)

Ethnicity, though, is a more recent, richer, and more accurate concept. It reflects the fact that what a person receives from his or her ancestors is a complex mix of culture and genetics. In terms of ethnography, non-Hispanic White Americans often do not refer to themselves as Whites. They are more likely to refer to themselves simply as Americans. Only when race is introduced as a specific topic do they resort uneasily to "White" and "Black" terminology.

In years past the term *Caucasian* was often used, but the word does not technically include the Celtic and Mediterranean peoples, who are today counted in that non-Hispanic White statistic in the census. We could call them European Americans, although this ignores the fact that

Hispanic culture has its roots in southern Europe and the term would meet with wide nonrecognition. We could call them "melted" Americans—those for whom the "melting pot" has worked and who consider themselves part of the mainstream of American culture—but this term actually includes many middle-class African-Americans, Hispanics, and Asians.

Some scholars have argued that we must deconstruct the concept of White people altogether. Yet we cannot, as a practical matter, ignore the fact that there is an ethnic majority or historic mainstream in American culture. The existence of this majority presents a set of realities, whether we like them or not, which impact upon leadership, evangelism, Christian education, and all other ministries of the church.

"Race as a category is usually applied to 'non-White' peoples," points out Michael W. Apple. "White people usually are not seen and named. They are centered as the human norm. 'Others' are raced; 'we' are just people." It is a fundamental reality that the ethnic majority in America has been raised for several generations with the unstated assumption that they and their culture are "regular American" or "normal." In fact, in a democratic tradition, without a multicultural ethic, the ideas and practices of the majority do become the norm.

The historic reality is that North America was settled several centuries ago by colonists from Britain, France, and other parts of northern Europe. These colonists destroyed almost all of the native civilization, importing what soon melded into a unitary culture, with the catalyst of emerging nationhood rooted in the Anglo Saxon (Western) cultural history. The English language, in the process, is fast becoming the common language, the modern "lingua franca," of the world.

A similar colonizing process, with the same cultural roots as well as a sense of connection to North America, has occurred in Australia and New Zealand, although those colonists did not import a slave population from Africa as did America.

This chapter is largely addressed to persons of color who find themselves providing leadership, within the Adventist Church and surrounding communities, over groups in which this Caucasian ethnic majority is included or, perhaps, comprises the majority or even the entire group. Because the Adventist Church is ethnically diverse, it is essential that leaders are able to function across cultural lines and in multicultural settings.

Because of all the factors noted above, and to make the text less complex to read, I will refer to the ethnic majority in North America simply as "Whites" and sometimes as "White Anglos." The observations that I make often apply equally to "melted" Americans who happen to be persons of color but share dominant features of the White mainstream American culture.

Understanding the White Experience

Although the baby bust generation (those Americans born from 1965 through 1980, sometimes called [disrespectfully, I believe] "Gen Xers") and the millennial generation (those born since 1980 through 1994) are increasingly multicultural in their experience, most Whites do not see the power relations between their privileged group and the ethnic minorities. To them, their culture is not only normal; it extends without limit until interrupted by something or someone different. It is common to speak of white paper as "blank." A room painted all white is seen as perhaps "needing a bit of color." It is the idea of whiteness as "neutrality," as "that which is not there," that is foundational to the White mind, but outside the awareness of most Whites.

Thus Whites take it for granted that their experience is the ordinary human experience, and this assumption undergirds the group's instincts toward other cultures and peoples. When this assumption is challenged, it can be for a White person exasperating and even threatening. For example, in a conversation a few years ago, a friend made reference to a certain local church and indicated that it was the only Adventist church in the city about which we were speaking. I pointed out that there were three African-American congregations and a Hispanic congregation in the city, and he responded with a "yes" in a tone of voice that suggested minor irritation. When I then added that the membership of those four congregations was, in fact, about five times the membership of the church he had mentioned, his tone of voice exhibited a hint of anger masking fear.

An ethical challenge can be assigned to Whites' assumption of their cultural experience as the norm. Yet the average person of any race will feel that he or she is being unfairly burdened with the misdeeds of his or her ancestors when such an analysis is introduced. Social ethical behavior over long periods of history is not a topic that nine out of 10 people understand, and the Adventist Church has done little to educate its members in this area.

If you are to exercise leadership over Whites, you must accept the reality that in daily practice most members of this group do not understand as racist their assumption that their experience is the norm. They do not see themselves as part of a privileged group, but simply as ordinary people. They will reject attempts to change their views on this unless those attempts are artfully designed and carefully paced.

This cultural and racial identity has been conferred by history upon Whites, and history will shape new identities for future generations of Whites, but right now this is reality. Whites are the ethnic majority in America. Their culture is the cultural mainstream. They experience their cultural dominance and privileged position as simply ordinary.

It must also be said that because of the cultural dominance of the White experience, and because of the extent to which the "mainstreaming" dynamic still works in America, as persons of color—immigrants and African-Americans—become increasingly middle class and achieve professional education and careers, they take on more of the characteristics described in this chapter. A historically African-American congregation that is today made up largely of professionals tends to behave more and more like a mainstream White congregation. The same is true of an immigrant congregation made up primarily of "the second generation."

Individualistic Values

The White experience is very individualistic. An African-American friend once asked me, "Why do Whites have such a hard time liking people of color?"

"You don't understand," I responded. "They don't dislike people of color any more than they dislike people in general. Frankly, Whites don't like anyone that much." I was attempting in a humorous way to explain the extreme individualism that has come to characterize White culture.

Daniel Boone is a hero of White American culture. A key part of the Boone legend is that as soon as he saw the smoke of another settler's fireplace, it was time for him to move on. The American poet Robert Frost wrote that "good fences make good neighbors." American settlers viewed Native Americans as uncivilized so long as they "roamed in bands," so they forced them to engage in the "civilized" farming of individual plots, even when attempts to learn such culturally foreign practices resulted in their near starvation.

This individuality is not all bad. It has given the world the concept of individual human rights, that each person is "endowed by his [or her] Maker with certain inalienable rights." This concept has provided individuals opportunity to achieve wealth and fame regardless of their background. In fact, our understanding of the Bible as teaching that each person has a personal relationship with God and the privilege of individual salvation issues in part from the ethic of individuality. So does our doctrine of individual accountability.

Yet in today's world the individualism ethic has been pushed to the farthest extreme yet seen in human history. It guides much of the White experience and spills over into other ethnic groups as well. Whites are less interested in group activities and social experience than other ethnic groups. They place less value on group solidarity and ties. For Whites, committees and business meetings are a necessary evil to be minimized and streamlined. To the extent that business can be conducted without formal meetings, leadership is seen as efficient and effective.

Fellowship activities are viewed as almost necessary evils—social forms to be honored only to the extent necessary to reassure everyone that "we are nice people," but seldom to be relished. White congregations are happy to have a fellowship dinner one Sabbath a month—of course, skipping a couple of summer months and maybe a month or two in the winter. They want to arrive for Sabbath school late and get out of worship promptly, and they do not understand cultures in which people remain at church all afternoon and into the evening.

Almost all Whites describe the worship of other ethnic groups as "long and emotional." They mention "all those amens" and are often not comfortable with the applause. You will know that your preaching is really connecting with a White congregation when it gets so silent that you can hear a pin drop! Reverence is defined as sitting silently, alone before God. Great European cathedrals feature empty space and small niches where individuals can pray alone.

White Adventists put much stock in stories about individuals who "read themselves into the message" completely without human contact. They like mission stories about converts who persisted in their newfound faith despite being disowned by their families and driven out by their communities. "Standing all alone for truth" is considered a highly valued experience. I once heard a well-known evangelist tell pastors, "You don't want to get too friendly with people you are studying with. I have found that if you get too friendly with them, they won't join the church." These are all ways of asserting a very individualistic set of values.

Whites prefer individual assignments rather than organizational structures. Recent generations are more accustomed to teamwork, but the White concept of teams has more to do with a "pecking order" than participatory democracy. Whites do not place a lot of value on persons expressing themselves, and actually ascribe more wisdom to those who keep silent in a meeting than to those who speak out "too much." Meetings are to be minimized; the real work is done by individuals, outside the meetings.

The White concept of individualism is tied also to certain ideas about "humility" and "modesty." Within White settings, and especially in cross-cultural or multicultural settings, it is considered best to keep oneself mostly hidden and never admit to a need for affirmation or empowerment. It is a violation of good manners to talk too much about one's background, achievements, or needs, or to put too much intensity into expressing one's views. It is not natural for Whites to be concerned that everyone in a group has the opportunity to express himself or herself, because it is assumed that those who have kept silent are doing a better job of self-control at the moment and are behaving in a way that is more acceptable than those who feel they must speak up.

Functioning as a Leader of Whites
Because of the highly individualistic values of the White culture, leadership may be more difficult to exercise in a Whites-dominated multicultural setting. Whites do not give their leaders as much immediate feedback as is true in some other cultures. They tend to sit back and expect leaders to perform "on their own," in a more individualistic way. They wait for leaders to come to them. They expect to be contacted individually and privately if the leader really wants their input or support.

An appeal for help from the pulpit will not successfully recruit many volunteers in a White congregation. It will be taken as an announcement, and the best and brightest workers will wait patiently to get a phone call, or until the leader initiates a private conversation. If no such contact is ever made, they may even complain privately to a friend, "I was not asked to help."

A general discussion of an important issue in a committee meeting or the church board will not necessarily surface all of the opinions and viewpoints of the members. It will be taken as an introduction to the topic, and key opinion makers in the group will wait for the leader to ask them privately for their views. The more volatile or complex the issue, the more this is true. In the most difficult and extreme circumstances, if the leader goes around the circle and asks each member of the committee by name to state his or her opinion, some will say, "I would rather not say." However, during a phone call or a one-on-one conversation in the parking lot following the meeting, those same individuals may pour out their hearts and express strong feelings on the topic at hand.

Listening is a particularly important skill for leaders working with White people. The one-on-one conversations with church members, fellow workers, etc., are more important than group discussions. It will take work to "dig out" what White people really think and feel; one should employ gentle, careful conversation that utilizes a subtle listening ability rather than interrogative interviewing skills.

To recognize these subtle signs, a great deal of cross-cultural learning is required. Sweat on the upper lip, the set of one's facial muscles, body language—all must be read within the cultural context. If you have grown up reading subconscious intent in the tone of voice and body language in one culture, you cannot expect to transport those subconscious understandings over to another culture. In most cases, you must relearn those codes through careful observation and disciplined listening.

An African-American friend and pastoral colleague who has pastored multicultural and White congregations says, "Listen to yourself, and in doing so, be prepared to learn differences between things that have been cultural assumptions and things that are true core values. Rather than insisting that you are heard, which is a demand that you place on others to enter into your experience and modes of communication, be certain that you are understood, which is a demand that you place on yourself to communicate through experiences and modes that will be effective with the listener."

To be a good listener does require self-control, but it does not mean that one must give up the moral authority or potential for proactive direction inherent in leadership. "This is not to say that you must disguise who you are," comments my colleague. That "is inauthentic and will ultimately undermine you, but . . . your first concern is to show that you understand who they are, which will then help them place a higher value on seeking to understand you." Leaders must show not only that they understand the other culture, but value that culture and experience as one equally valid with the leader's own.

"For example, you can tease a congregation for not responding to your preaching with hearty amens if you are a guest speaker, but if they hear that week after week, then they will perceive that you have judged their comfort level as falling short of what is acceptable." You need to ask yourself, my colleague points out, "Are you asking them to blare out responses to get more out of your sermon, or to just make you feel better about your preaching?"

To be heard privately and individually is the highest value among Whites, and to have that expression kept as private as possible. In other words, when you as a leader share what you have heard, it is important to mask its individual origins and reword it so that it is a "disembodied" or "objective" concept or viewpoint when it is brought into the group.

Leadership functions differently in White culture, so assumptions gained from what you may have learned previously about leadership techniques may be invalid. In addition, there may be huge differences in the expectations of leaders in different cultures. These expectations must be learned in order to be effective.

Whites generally expect leadership to be exercised behind the scenes as much as possible. Their greatest respect is reserved for leaders who have a modest, self-effacing style, who act as if leadership has been thrust upon them almost against their will. At the same time, leaders are expected to accomplish much without being visible, without using authority, and without much affirmation.

Some differences in expectations about leadership and how it is exercised relate more to class than to ethnicity. A "white-collar congregation" in which most of the members are highly educated and work in professional and management occupations will expect their pastor to exercise leadership in a different style than will a typical "blue-collar congregation." This holds true regardless of the ethnic profile of a congregation, but is particularly true among congregations made up entirely or primarily of Whites.

In a blue-collar congregation a leader is expected to function as the boss. He is expected to state clearly what needs to be done, make assignments, and see that everyone gets to work. There may be time for questions and answers, but no one expects a debate. At times there may be those who challenge the leader and disagree with his or her directions, but he or she is expected to show strength and command loyalty.

On the other hand, in a white-collar congregation a leader is expected to function as a facilitator and encourage teamwork. Decisions are to be made collectively, with the group members having opportunity to pool their ideas and engage in brainstorming. There may be a variety of views about which direction the group should take, but it is considered best if the leader remains somewhat neutral until the group comes to an impasse and asks for the leader to assert some direction. Even then, if the leader selects a direction that lacks support, the group is unlikely to implement the decision, even if they vote it.

Whites expect leaders to be sensitive to these subtle clues about class and to act accordingly. They are offended by a leader who does not understand the different approaches and cannot shift his or her style accordingly.

Dealing With White Fears

Many Whites in a multicultural setting will be reticent to speak out, to get involved, to push forward their input. Rather they are much more likely to sit back, to let others do the talking, and then to go home and feel left out.

Whites who find it necessary to participate in open discussions of cross-cultural issues in multicultural settings often go away with such profound feelings of uneasiness that they begin to think of leaving the congregation or institution. "I felt like I was forced to undress," one veteran denominational employee told me concerning his experience during a difficult confrontation between ethnic groups in his congregation. "I can never feel comfortable in that group again." Within six months he accepted a call to another institution even though for years he had told me that he was thinking of retiring there. I could cite many other examples of this uneasiness, which fuels the social phenomena called "White flight."

Because Whites are used to being in the majority (one of the privileges of being White), they often simply do not know what to do or say when that privileged position is challenged. Whites do not grow up learning how to be in the minority. Consequently, when a White person is placed in the position of being in the minority in a congregation, committee, or other situation in which people of color make up the majority, he or she is likely to clam up and withdraw.

Fear is related to the unknown, and to be thrust into a minority situation is an unknown circumstance to most Whites. This fear is, at times, exacerbated by the way the public media have manipulated White fears by associating young African-American and Hispanic males with crime and violence. But the essential fear of being put into an unknown situation is there in any case.

The church and leaders of all races have not helped Adventist Whites to prepare themselves for the new demographic realities. For example, my father attended an academy in the Midwest that was "lily White," without any persons of color among the students, faculty, or staff. I attended an integrated academy in the early 1960s, as did most baby boomers, in which there were a handful of African-Americans, Hispanics, and Asians among an overwhelming majority of Whites, and no person of color held an adult position of authority. My two daughters attended an academy in which Whites were only about 20-25 percent of the student body and the principal was an African-American, the guidance counselor Hispanic, etc. Obviously, my daughters' experience with ethnic diversity is far different from most in my generation and almost everyone in my father's generation.

White fears must be addressed clearly and sensitively in order to prevent "White flight," as well as to achieve God's goal of a church in which "there is neither Jew nor Greek, bond or slave, male nor female." Whites cannot simply be expected to understand, to know how to fit in. In fact, minorities in America know much more about White culture than Whites know about minority cultures. Part of the reality of being a minority person is being exposed every day to a culture dominated by the majority. The majority, on the other hand, can turn a blind eye to the minority groups and their cultures.

In fact, the "color-blind" approach to race relations is the favorite of most Whites. They like it, I believe, because it certainly seems just while at the same time being simple and straightforward. They are rescued from the complications of learning about other cultures and learning to be sensitive to the ethnic and cultural backgrounds of individuals. If they can treat a person of color just like they would another White person, then they do not have to learn anything new or experience any situations that are new to them.

The subtle dimension of racism involved in the color-blind approach is simply lost on most Whites in America. Many consciously assume that White is better and to be preferred by people of color, in which case it is preferential to treat them just like they would other Whites—they just don't examine this assumption. They assume that White is "normal" because it represents the traditional majority experience.

In order to get White Adventists to understand the latent racism of the color-blind approach, to learn from values inherent in other cultures, church leaders must be intentional about helping them deal with their fears. We must be willing to "name the fears" in settings that provide opportunity for careful thinking and dialogue. We must make these settings as comfortable as possible and allow the quality time necessary to help people think rationally about things that are so fearful to them that they will take any excuse to avoid them.

It is a mistake to dismiss White fears as silly, immature, or racist. Obviously, these fears have elements of all of those dimensions. Fear always connects with our baser emotions. Yet there is a reality here that triggers the fear—Whites are being asked to move beyond their comfort zone into the unknown, into a world of difference.

Empowering White Church Growth and Outreach

The White church is not growing in North America or anywhere else on the globe, except perhaps in some areas of the former Soviet Union. In many of the large cities in North America and Europe, although the majority of the general population is made up of indigenous Whites, the overwhelming majority of Seventh-day Adventists are people of color and immigrants. One recent study of the New York City metropolitan region (including the suburbs in New Jersey and Connecticut) indicated that of the 200 Adventist congregations in that area, no more than one or two has a majority of White, nonimmigrant members.

In these major urban areas, the White work is actually dying. The White membership that does exist has a much higher average age than the overall membership; few White youths are growing up with, in these churches, and White young adults moving to the cities find it almost impossible to connect with a congregation that meets their needs. Very few Whites are being baptized, and it is almost impossible to get the most skilled White pastors to come to these churches, with the result that area conference leaders are no longer making real efforts to recruit such skilled White pastors.

Unless administrators and pastors of color take the lead in promoting and empowering White outreach and church growth in these cities, the work will not be finished and the mission of the Adventist Church will not be achieved. The missionary spirit that has motivated generations of White leaders to sacrifice to plant the Adventist Church among other cultures at home and around the world must now flow back to benefit the White work in America and other historically White majority countries. African-American and Hispanic conference presidents must be willing to hire White pastors and commission them to plant White and multiethnic congregations in unreached communities.

They must be willing to risk aggressively recruiting strong White leaders to come to their fields and empower work among Whites. To do any less is to be unfaithful to the message and mission of the Seventh-day Adventist Church.

For further reading:

Noel Ignatiev, *How the Irish Became White.* New York: Routledge, 1995.

Richard Dyer, *White.* New York: Routledge, 1997; and Michelle Fine, Lois Weis, Linda Powell, and L. Mun Wong, eds., *Off White: Readings on Race, Power, and Society.* New York: Routledge, 1997.

Kincheloe et al, eds., *White Reign.* New York: St. Martin's Press, 1998.

CAN MEN LEAD WOMEN MORE EFFECTIVELY?

Seven Common Mistakes and How to Avoid Them

By Kit Watts, M.A.

Director Women's Resource Center, La Sierra University,
with Karen Coy Darnell, M.A.

How can men lead women more effectively? No one denies that biological differences between males and females exist, but many leaders and managers have been caught flatfooted, assuming biology is destiny. Many thought men should become doctors, while women should be only nurses.

Today we know that the professional differences between men and women are far fewer than we once believed, and the gap is closing. In the United States, where growing numbers of people prize egalitarianism, women succeed in careers once considered the private domain of men—law, medicine, politics, science, management, business, and pastoral ministry.

Yet because many men and women grow up being socialized differently, we often expect different things from them. Men have often been expected to put money, status, and job promotions first in life, while women have often been expected to keep house and mind the children. A growing number of North American men, however, want careers that do not continually deny them time with their families. And a vast number of women take pride in their career achievements.

This chapter is a reality check. What incorrect assumptions do some men have about women? What stereotypes cause some male leaders to reduce or even stymie the productivity and leadership potential of women? This chapter describes seven common problem areas. It also offers antidotes. These recommendations are not exhaustive, but they are concrete steps others have tried and found successful. Consider them.

Common Mistakes

1. False assumptions about family priorities. Many leaders have assumed that because women may bear children, they are undesirable, undependable employees. In fact, women make up nearly half (46 percent) of the workforce in the U.S. and 36 percent of the worldwide labor force.[1] If they were to withdraw from the workplace, the economy would go into a tailspin.

Furthermore, women in the workplace respond to family issues in diverse ways. Jennifer, a hospital manager for 10 years, delivered her first child at 8:30 a.m. and held a budget meeting in her hospital room at 3:30 p.m. Michelle took five months maternity leave, as allowed by the Family and Medical Leave Act, passed in 1993 in the United States. Kelly, who is single and has no children, has worked daily since she graduated from college more than 30 years ago.

Is it true that mothers are unreliable workers and women who become pregnant will not return to the workforce? Recent statistics show that women are able to cope with both children and careers. Forty percent of working women in the U.S. have children under age 18. In 1995 only 17 percent of new mothers chose not to return to the workforce. In other words, 83 percent did return within six months. A survey of senior female executives showed 72 percent are married and 64 percent have children.

Women have learned to balance work and family. Recent studies indicate that women suffer less "work-to-family" and "family-to-work" conflicts than men do.[2] Furthermore, successful mothers (and fathers) learn coping strategies at home and carry them into the workplace to benefit the employer. Such strategies include establishing priorities, developing positive attitudes, and increasing efficiency.

2. *Productivity drops as the workplace adjusts to families.* Many assume that regimentation is essential to productivity. As a result, many managers resist making adjustments that would benefit mothers and fathers of small children.

Today most parents work. Only 17 percent of families in America have a stay-at-home mom and a working dad. Employers have found that alternative work arrangements, such as flextime, either do not affect an employee's performance, or actually improve it. Other adjustments that benefit parents such as customizing a career path, pacing advancement, giving employees more control over their own work, and allowing them to work independently may actually improve a company's bottom line over time.

Flextime is most successful when coupled with good childcare. Mothers without convenient childcare are twice as likely to quit their jobs as those who have nearby childcare. Unfortunately, childcare during late or early hours or on weekends is hard to find. Yet, one third of working poor mothers work on weekends.[3]

Workplace adjustments seem to help everyone. A 1991 report observes that "organizations need to change the work environment to make it easier for women to pursue a productive and challenging career and for men to contribute more fully to their families' development."[4]

Leadership success key: A skilled leader will recognize that not all women have families and will not relate to them in the same way. He or she will also recognize that organizations retain good employees by having good benefits. For mothers and fathers of young children, good childcare and flextime will improve their productivity and increase the chance that they will stay with the employer.

2. False assumptions about women's abilities. For centuries most cultures have assumed that women are inferior to men intellectually, physically, and emotionally. This has led employers and educators to give preference to men and discriminate against women.

Western society is changing. In 1960 only one quarter of American women with young children stayed home full-time. Fifty percent of women held part-time jobs, and another 25 percent (mainly African-American, Hispanic, and poor women) worked full-time while also caring for young children.[5]

Elsewhere in the world, women have held jobs that Americans would consider unusual. The majority of chimney sweeps in Austria, most doctors in Russia, and the larger number of road builders in India are women.

Given the opportunity, women are often competent leaders. An Australian study showed employees ranked women managers equal to men. Workers said women leaders were well able to articulate a vision, use lateral or nontraditional thinking, encourage workers' development, use participative decision-making, and promote a cooperative work environment.[6]

Women use recognized leadership skills almost twice as often as men, according to one study of U.S. teachers. They engaged students in cooperative learning and group projects, and allowed students to select topics and to evaluate one another's work.[7]

The glass ceiling. False assumptions die hard. Despite women's demonstrated leadership abilities, men still occupy 96 percent of America's top corporate jobs. Middle-management positions are more evenly distributed, but women are paid less. Although women held 49 percent of managerial and professional specialty occupations in 1997, salaries of men and women of various ethnic groups were dramatically different.

	WHITE	ASIAN/OTHER	AFRICAN-AMERICAN	HISPANIC
MEN	$1.00	$0.91	$0.65	$0.65
WOMEN	$0.59	$0.67	$0.58	$0.48

Leaders must recognize their own ethnic biases. Motorola spent six years promoting women on the vice presidential track only to realize that nearly all of those promoted were White. Since 1995 the company has become proactive with women of color. Of 54 women vice presidents, 11 are now women of color.

What will help women demonstrate their skills and achieve promotions? Women of color report that they succeeded when they gained access to high-visibility assignments, performed above expectations, communicated well, and had an influential mentor.

Leadership success key: A skilled leader will give women the opportunity to grow and succeed. For those aspiring to leadership, give high-visibility assignments and the mentoring needed to succeed. A woman benefits when mentored by a senior man in her field and a woman of her own ethnicity from any area.

3. False assumptions about women's productivity and career goals. Some leaders have assumed that women would not work as hard as men. Some also believe women do not aspire to leadership.

Research shows that women are actually more concerned than men with task accomplishment.[8] Women often complain that they have to work harder than men to prove their worth.

Studies also reveal that women leaders derive much satisfaction from their achievements.[9] When women are denied the chance to achieve while men in the same career are given that opportunity, women have lower job satisfaction than their counterparts.[10]

What happens when motivated women are denied recognition and achievement? For one thing, it accelerates the rate at which women leave a job to begin their own businesses. In the 1980s women started businesses at six times the rate of men.[11]

One company's proactive experiment. Proctor & Gamble discovered in 1991 that two of every three good performers who quit the company were women. In exit interviews, many women said they wanted to spend more time with their families. Of the 50 contacted later, however, only two had actually left the workforce. Many had accepted high-profile, high-stress jobs.

Proctor & Gamble chose to set a "market share" goal of 40 percent for women in management. (This matched the percentage of women students at the schools where Proctor & Gamble recruited.) The company also repackaged benefits, launched internal advertising campaigns, and began a Mentor Up program, in which younger women taught older men about women's issues. Five years later women held nearly one third of the vice presidential and general managerial positions.[12]

Do such changes benefit only women, or do they also help the company? Lewis Platt, president and CEO of Hewlett-Packard, stated that his company's revenues had doubled and profits tripled along with a fourfold increase of women executives.

Leadership success key: The skilled executive will recognize that many women work hard and will reward women who show initiative. Many women enjoy leadership and succeed as leaders. Position your company or organization to take advantage of their talents, and that should greatly improve productivity.

4. Failure to recognize different communication and leadership styles. Many leaders are unaware that men and women tend to lead differently. These differences decrease as society becomes more egalitarian. Yet because men traditionally have held dominant roles and women have been subordinate to them, different styles have been common. Of course, factors other than gender affect how a person leads—including personality type and learning styles.

Communication research shows that historic male leadership reflects competition, aggression, and control styles to those in dominant roles. Women leaders tend to share information and power—a skill that may say more about being subordinate than about being female. In today's new business environment, however, sharing information and power is seen as a positive leadership trait for both men and women.

Managers who fail to recognize different leadership and communication styles may overlook excellent skills that women may bring to the workplace. For example, women police officers use less-combative techniques to arrest offenders. Margaret York, a policewoman in Los Angeles, has the highest confession rate in the homicide division.[13]

Good leaders capitalize on a person's strengths, whether male or female. The skillful interpersonal communication women often exhibit can improve group participation, inspire enthusiasm for work, and preserve good relationships. On the other hand, the assertiveness, independence, competitiveness, and confidence that men often exhibit can position one's company favorably in the marketplace. Organizations need workers with all of these skills.

Some leaders have trouble understanding a communication style different from his or her own. If a man asks assertively for resources to do his job and a woman asks with deference, the manager must choose to provide resources based on strategic goals, not on communication styles.

Leadership success key: Since as a result of socialization, men and women tend to use language differently, the skilled manager will learn to lead and speak in ways with which women will respond positively. Recognize the value of both male and female styles of communication and leadership, and allow women to build on their strengths to accomplish your goals.

5. Failure to understand different responses to stress. Anyone who works experiences stress. Studies indicate, however, that women perceive their work environments as much more hostile than men. They see less opportunity for advancement and find fewer mentors. Women often encounter sexist attitudes and comments. Male coworkers often leave women out of informal socializing. Yet many women are reluctant to complain and be seen as troublemakers.[14]

One common response to stress is anger. Men tend to express anger externally by raising their voices and engaging in heated argument. At times they become physically aggressive.

Women tend to internalize anger and frustration by absorbing it, by expressing feelings, or at times, by crying. Because many men see tears as a sign of weakness, women employees may lose credibility in their eyes.

Men generally feel safe expressing their anger openly. Women seldom do because of social stigma, especially in the presence of men. If women do express anger openly, they are often rejected as not being feminine. After a stress-producing episode, however, women who swallowed their anger may "get back" at a manager using indirect aggression. Indirect aggression may be as subtle as "forgetting" to mail an important document or as catastrophic as wiping out the company's database.

To recognize and defuse stress in the workplace, a manager must first recognize and defuse his or her own stress. Leaders set the tone. When they deal with their personal and professional issues in a functional manner, they provide a model for employees.

Managers must also treat employees with respect, giving reprimands in private and providing honest, compassionate answers when questions are raised. A service that helps diffuse stress in the workplace is a confidential counseling service provided as part of the health plan.

Leadership success key: The skilled leader will learn to recognize and defuse stressful situations. Acknowledge anger as an emotion felt by both men and women. Don't assume that crying shows weakness; recognize that it is one way to relieve pressure. By treating it neutrally (sharing a tissue), a manager encourages the employee to move on and become more productive.

6. Failure to take sexual harassment seriously. Because women have often held subordinate positions in the workplace, male managers have sometimes abused their power by seeking sexual contact with female employees. Laws in the United States define sexual harassment as a form of sex discrimination that violates Title VII of the Civil Rights Act of 1964 (and the 1991 amendments to that act).

Sexual harassment includes requests for sexual favors or "other verbal or physical conduct of a sexual nature" when "submission to or rejection of this conduct explicitly or implicitly affects an individual's employment, unreasonably interferes with an individual's work performance, or creates an intimidating, hostile, or offensive work environment."[15]

Many organizations have policies in place to deal with sexual harassment complaints. However, studies show that men and women may respond to complaints from workers in different ways. Women managers are more likely than men to follow the company procedures adopted for dealing with sexual harassment.[16]

Leadership success key: The skilled leader will take sexual harassment complaints seriously and follow established procedures for addressing concerns. Such action will confirm the integrity of your leadership.

7. Assumptions about how others view women. Many managers assume customers and coworkers will reject women leaders. Scholars call this "rational bias." In other words, "individuals who do not themselves hold negative prejudices may nonetheless 'rationally' choose to discriminate," believing they are protecting their organization from misunderstanding.[17] Those with "rational bias" resort to such explanations as "We must consider the customs and cultural views of our international clients, like the Arabs," or "In my experience, customers prefer to deal with men."

When people actually see women in action, they often have positive experiences. A study of 117 Caucasian men and women attending evening business classes at Tel Aviv University in Israel revealed that both men and women who had previously worked for a woman would almost always choose to hire a woman for an available management position. Those who had not previously worked for a woman were evenly divided over whether they would select a man or a woman for the job.[18]

Research among college students has shown that they usually rate male and female teachers equally. When differences are found, more favor women than men.[19]

Leadership success key: The skilled leader will give competent women high-visibility assignments that allow customers and coworkers to observe them in action. In this way, you will empower female leadership.

Conclusion

Women are similar to men in many ways. Women differ from men in other ways. Successful leaders recognize these similarities and differences and adjust for them. Good managers give all employees the opportunity to succeed.

Effective managers know that when their employees succeed, they succeed. Supporting one's employees, whether men or women, improves morale, increases productivity, and promotes the success of the organization.

---

[1] Worldwide statistics cited in this chapter but otherwise uncredited are from Joni Seager, *The State of Women in the World Atlas*, 2ed. (London: Penguin Books, 1997). United States statistics cited in this chapter but otherwise uncredited came from Catalyst, an organization that began in 1962 as a career resource center for women. Catalyst researches the status of women in the workplace and advises organizations "to enable professional women to achieve their maximum potential and help employers capitalize on the talents of their female employees." The Internet holds more information at *http://www.catalystwomen.org/press.html*. Statistics not otherwise identified refer to the United States.

[2] Catherine Kirchmeyer, "Nonwork-to-Work Spillover: A More Balanced View of the Experiences and Coping of Professional Women and Men," *Sex Roles* 28 (1993): 531-549; and Eagly, *Journal of Social Psychology*, 1998.

[3] Los Angeles *Times*, Aug. 1, 1999.

[4] Linda E. Duxbury and Christopher A. Higgins, "Gender Differences in Work-Family Conflict," *Journal of Applied Psychology* 76, No. 1 (1991): 71.

[5] Mary Frances Berry, *The Politics of Parenthood: Child Care, Women's Rights, and the Myth of the Good Mother* (New York: Viking, 1993), p. 7.

[6] Sally A. Carless, "Gender Differences in Transformational Leadership: An Examination of Superior, Leader, and Subordinate Perspectives," *Sex Roles* 39 (1998): 887-899.

[7] Helen Astin, *Women in Higher Education*, March 1992.

[8] Alice H. Eagly and Blair T. Johnson, "Gender and Leadership Style: A Meta-Analysis,"

Psychological Bulletin 108 (1990): 233-248.

[9] Lynn R. Offermann and Cheryl Beil, "Toward an Understanding of Women and Leadership," *Psychology of Women Quarterly* 16 (1992): 37-52.

[10] Charlotte Chiu, "Do Professional Women Have Lower Job Satisfaction Than Professional Men? Lawyers as a Case Study," *Sex Roles* 38 (1998): 521-533.

[11] Anne M. Morrison and Mary Ann Von Glinow, "Women and Minorities in Management," *American Psychologist,* February 1990, pp. 200, 201.

[12] Tara Parker-Pope, "Inside P&G, A Pitch to Keep Women Employees," *Wall Street Journal,* Sept. 9, 1998.

[13] Judy B. Rosener, *America's Competitive Secret: Women Managers* (New York: Oxford University Press, 1995), pp. 131, 132.

[14] Joseph Stokes, Stephanie Riger, and Megan Sullivan, "Measuring Perceptions of the Working Environment for Women in Corporate Settings," *Psychology of Women Quarterly* 19 (1995): 533-537.

[15] Online information is available at *http://www.eeoc.gov.*

[16] DeeAnn N. Gehlauf and Paula M. Popovich, "The Effects of Personal and Situational Factors on University Administrators' Responses to Sexual Harassment," *Research in Higher Education* 35 (1994): 373-383.

[17] Susan Trentham and Laurie Larwood, "Gender Discrimination and the Workplace: An Examination of Rational Bias Theory," *Sex Roles* 38 (1998): 2.

[18] Asya Pazy, "Sex-Linked Bias in Promotional Decisions," *Psychology of Women Quarterly* 16 (1992): 213-223.

[19] Kenneth A. Feldman, "College Students' Views of Male and Female College Teachers: Part II—Evidence From Students' Evaluations of Their Classroom Teachers," *Research in Higher Education* 34 (1993).

For further reading:

Catalyst. *Advancing Women in Business: The Catalyst Guide to Best Practices From the Corporate Leaders.* San Francisco: Jossey-Bass Publishers, 1998.

DeLaat, Jacqueline. *Gender in the Workplace: A Case Study Approach.* Thousand Oaks, Calif.: Sage Publications, 1999.

Ricci, Laura. *Twelve Views From Women's Eyes: Managing the New Majority.* Austin, Tex.: R3, 1997.

Rosener, Judy B. *America's Competitive Secret: Women Managers.* New York: Oxford University Press, 1995.

Audios:

Carlson, Richard. *Don't Sweat the Small Stuff at Work.* Simon and Schuster Audio, 1999.

Gill, Deborah Menken. *The Biblical Liberated Woman.* Addresses the biblical texts regarding the status of women and is relevant to the workplace. Can be obtained through Christians for Biblical Equality at (612) 872-6898, or *http://www.cbeinternational.org*.

McKenna, Colleen. *Powerful Communication Skills.* Random House Audio Books, 1998.

Web sites

Catalyst: *http://www.catalystwomen.org*

Links to Web sites of interest to women in business:

   http://umbc7.umbc.edu/~korenman/wmst/links_bus.html

Links to Web sites of interest to women's studies in general:

   http://umbc7.umbc.edu/~korenman/wmst/links.html

ELLEN WHITE'S VISION OF CROSS-CULTURAL MINISTRY: DIVERSITY PRINCIPLES FOR A CHURCH IN A NEW MILLENNIUM

By Leslie N. Pollard, D.Min., Ph.D.

Candidate, Vice President for Diversity,
Loma Linda University Adventist Health Sciences Center

On October 27-30, 1999, the North American Division convened a historic summit on the theme "Modeling the Ministry of Christ: Racial Harmony in the New Millennium." More than 350 leaders, laypersons, administrators, and teachers from the North American Division gathered to explore ways that the racial witness of the church can be enhanced and improved in the twenty-first century. The NAD Office of Human Relations stated: "The purpose of the summit is to bring leaders of the Seventh-day Adventist Church together, not in confrontation, but in trust, to listen carefully and respectfully to each other and to the whole faith community, to search for solutions, focusing on what is right rather than who is right, and to hold ourselves and the church accountable in areas where change is needed." That the NAD is openly and positively discussing racial issues is a significant sign of progress, since sensitive racial issues are often at the core of interaction between different racial groups.

Clearly, the North American Division's 1998 membership of 868,070 is one of the most racially diverse in the world church. And between 1990 and the year 2000, predictions are that the diversity of the NAD will increase (see graph showing NAD racial/ethnic demographics).

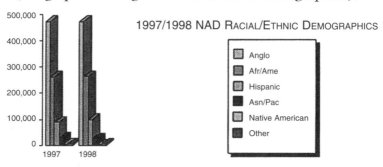

1997/1998 NAD RACIAL/ETHNIC DEMOGRAPHICS

Anglo
Afr/Ame
Hispanic
Asn/Pac
Native American
Other

On a personal note, I have had the privilege of conducting numerous diversity workshops for denominational employees and general church members. During these sessions a noticeable openness to exploring how the racial history of the United States during the past 300 years has affected the church's ministry and mission is evident. Building on those observations, I submit that any discussion of racial harmony in the North American Division must explore the principle-based guidance that we find in Ellen White's most challenging and comprehensive diversity statement.

In the nineteenth century, Ellen White's concerns centered in the relationship between America's Whites and the recently released "Colored" people. As with the other inspired writers, the principles identified by Ellen White apply to relationships between all people groups. While the central concern of her statement is a discussion of the relationship between Black persons and White persons in America at the turn of the nineteenth century, the principles that she articulated universalize her counsel and make it relevant wherever racial harmony is sought. If we allow the Lord to bless our witness in the area of racial harmony, then the work of the North American Division will be greatly enhanced (see John 17:20, 21).

On Sabbath March 21, 1891, Mrs. White delivered a staggering challenge to 30 leaders of the General Conference of Seventh-day Adventists. She had and would address the issue of race in her writings (see *Testimonies,* vol. 1, pp. 254, 258, 259, 264-268; vol. 7, pp. 220-230; vol. 9, pp. 199-226). But the March 21, 1891, presentation signaled a comprehensive call both to repentance and specific action by the leaders of the church. Leaders and laity were standing face to face with the unavoidable challenge of applying the claims of the cross to the racially polarized United States. Modern Adventist audiences are often surprised to learn that Mrs. White's General Conference sermon is comprehensive in its application of Scriptural teaching and social insight. Centered on principle, her approach to racial harmony provides the basis for the creation of a cross-centered culture in which the values of service, mission, and mutuality prevail. It is only by the creation of this transcendent cross culture that we will experience and sustain a satisfying and effective church unity in the Seventh-day Adventist fellowship. I encourage every member of the North American Division to prayerfully read her sermon in its entirety.

Race in Nineteenth-Century America:
The Social Context of Ellen White's Sermon

Less than 50 years after America's founding, in 1776, the country was transformed from a nation of immigrants to a stratified society in which racial hierarchy shaped social interaction. In the nineteenth-century world in which the Seventh-day Adventist Church was born, this social hierarchy was fueled by "scientific racism," that body of racial description and categorization informed by the biological and social research of the eighteenth and nineteenth centuries. Scientific racism emerged from European and American attempts to analyze, understand, and classify the world within the recently created domain called science. Exploration, analysis, and investigation of the natural world required methods based on hypothesis, testing observation, and analysis.[1] The empirical pursuit of knowledge that emerged by the end of the eighteenth century appealed to the so-called rational mind of man. Between the years 1700 to 1900, science played an important role in convincing the world that "savages" were biologically inferior to the members of civilized societies.

The first major scientist to attempt racial classification was Carolus Linnaeus, whose *Systamae Naturae* in 1735 divided humanity into Homo Europaeus, Homo Asiaticus, Homo Africanus, and Homo Americanus. By the nineteenth century, Georges Cuvier postulated a three-part division of humanity into Caucasians, Mongolians, and Negroes.[2] Anthropologists such as Samuel Morton, Josiah Nott, and George Gliddon influenced public opinion about race through their major research and publications. Morton, a Philadelphia physician, amassed the largest collection of human skulls known at that time.

Interestingly, when early Adventists were focusing on the intercessory ministry of Jesus Christ, Morton was publishing *Crania Americana; or, a Comparative View of the Skulls of Various Aboriginal Nations of North and South America* (1839) and *Crania Aegyptica; or, Observations on Egyptian Ethnography; Derived From Anatomy, History, and the Monuments* (1844). In these works on craniology, Morton linked cranial capacity to intellectual and moral aptitude. He placed the Caucasian at the top of a pyramid of intelligence and capability and the Negro at the bottom of the pyramid. Josiah Nott, an understudy of Morton's, asserted the natural inferiority of the Negro in an effort to assist the pro-slavery forces of the nineteenth century. He argued that Negroes were like children, best served by American enslavement.

In 1854 Nott and Gliddon, both close disciples of Morton, published *Types of Mankind,* a "scientific" book that documented variations among human species. Its findings were used to support pro-slavery arguments by slavery supporters. *Types of Mankind* went through 10 editions by the end of the nineteenth century and became one of that century's most influential texts on anthropology.

Scientific racism also became codified in certain legal decisions. Probably the most significant legal decision to confirm the social and legal inferiority of the American Negro was the Dred Scott decision of 1857. The majority opinion, written by Chief Justice Roger B. Taney, detailed how "far below" Whites Negroes were "in the scale of created beings" and that the Constitution guaranteed them no rights. Unfortunately, out of scientific and legal findings were created racial hierarchies: a societal "chain of being" and other notions of racial inferiority that provided the imperical and legal bases for justifying existing color-based social stratification. Higher criticism also undermined the Genesis account of Creation by proposing hierarchical concepts of polygenesis (multiple creation acts for the various races). These ideas provided a religious rationale for the preservation of racial hierarchy.

Thus the social acceptability of scientific racism along with the economic demands of a society in need of cheap labor provided the basis for a specific thinking about the Negro. Chancellor William Harper said in 1837 that "the Negro race, from their temperament and capacity, are particularly suited to the [slave] situation which they occupy."[3] In an address to the United States Senate, James Hammond explained that "in all social systems, there must be a class to do the menial duties, to perform the drudgery of life. This is a class requiring but a low order of intellect and but little skill. . . . Fortunately for the South, she found a race adapted to that purpose. We call them slaves."[4] In 1861 Alexander Stephens, a pro-slavery writer, declared, "With us, all the White race, however high or low, rich or poor, are equal in the eyes of the law. Not so with the Negro. Subordination is his place."[5]

Stephen Douglas, presidential contender against Abraham Lincoln, argued that "the civilized world has always held that when any race of men have shown themselves to be so degraded by ignorance, superstition, cruelty, and barbarism, as to be utterly incapable of governing themselves, they must, in the nature of things, be governed by others, by such laws as are deemed to be applicable to their condition."[6] Thomas Huxley, philosopher, scientist, and defender of Charles Darwin, wrote: "No rational man, cognizant of the facts, believes that the average Negro is the equal, still less the superior of the average White man."[7]

Such social constructs provided the basis in the nineteenth century for the social and legal separation of the races, the subjugation of the Negro, laws against miscegenation, a lack of national commitment to the education of its "colored people," and the refusal to regard the Negro as an equal, despite the Thirteenth, Fourteenth, and Fifteenth Amendments to the constitution.[8] This is the social context of her sermon. How would she respond? What would Mrs. White teach on the matter of race relations?

Ellen White's Call to Cross-Culture: Race and the Church

Ellen White was born a child of nineteenth-century America. Born in Gorham, Maine, in 1827, her earliest years were spent in the Methodist Church, a congregation divided over the Negro question. While many of her neighbors were free Negroes, she also associated with William Foy as a teenager.[9] She became a part of the Millerite movement in the 1840s, married James White at 17, and left the Millerites after the great disappointment of October 22, 1844.

She took up her prophetic ministry in 1844 at 17 years of age while popular notions regarding the biological, social, and civilizational inferiority of the Negro were commonly accepted. By 1860, fully after E. G. White had practiced her ministry for approximately 15 years, the total number of slaves in the United States had exceeded 4 million.[10] She lived through the existence of slavery, through its abolition in 1865, and through the founding of the Seventh-day Adventist Church in 1863.

While the Civil War ended slavery, it did not end the social servitude of Black persons. As one writer said: "The North may have won the War, but the South won the peace." By the Battle Creek General Conference of 1891, it is safe to say that the Seventh-day Adventist Church was at best ambivalent concerning its responsibility to Black persons, and at worst the church was recalcitrant. This is clear from a reading of Mrs. White's sermon. By 1891, somewhere between 4 and 5 million unreached "Colored" people sat in the living room of Seventh-day Adventist mission like a white elephant. Mrs. White concluded that the collective refusal of Seventh-day Adventist leadership to address the racial situation in the Seventh-day Adventist Church could not continue, thus, at 64 years of age, she decided to speak to the issue in a forthright, uncompromising manner. Mrs. White's sermon can be divided into three sections: the cross-centered basis for a new direction, the recent actions and present condition of the church, and the challenge of Christ-centered, grace-filled mission.

An Analysis of the Sermon

Ellen G. White presented "Our Duty to the Colored People" at Battle Creek,

Michigan, on March 21, 1891. She opened by declaring, "There has been much perplexity as to how our laborers in the South shall deal with the color line. It has been a question to some how far to concede to the prevailing prejudice against the Colored people. *The Lord has given us light concerning all such matters. There are principles laid down in His Word that should guide us in dealing with these perplexing questions"* (italics supplied).

Mrs. White opens her sermon with a hermeneutical announcement. She will not rely on the "science" or law of her day, but identifies the principles in Scripture that make the creation of a new culture of service, mission, and mutuality imperative. Her appeal is biblically and morally grounded. But this scriptural appeal is not a fundamentalist's interpretation of Scripture; otherwise she could not have supported resistance to slavery.[11] Note that Ellen White calls for a principle-centered approach to the problems of race, prejudice, bigotry, and discrimination. She is keenly aware that this approach is transformative.

Consider her sermonic assertions to the General Conference and the principles she used to disable the discrimination in her nineteenth-century church. These same principles will guide us today as we plan for positive racial witness in a globally connected church. Since in one article it is impossible to exhaust the richness and depth of her discourse, the following statements are illustrative.

E. G. White Challenge	Diversity Principles
"The Lord Jesus came to our world to save men and women of all nationalities. He died as much for the Colored people as for the White race."	The universality of Christ's mission on the accessibility of Christ's atonement are for all people. John 3:16; Matthew 28:18.
"The Redeemer of the world was of humble parentage. He the Majesty of heaven, the King of glory, humbled Himself to accept humanity, and then He chose a life of poverty and toil."	The message of the doctrine of the Incarnation imparts dignity to the humble and poverty stricken in society. Philippians 2:1-10.
"He did not associate with the leaders of the nation. He dwelt among the lowly of the earth. To all appearances He was merely a humble man, with few friends."	The sacrificial condescension of the earthly Jesus is to remind us that Christ chose the outcast and the marginalized for His associates. Philippians 2:7, 8.

(Chart continued on next page)

E. G. White Challenge	Diversity Principles
"With Him there is no respect of persons. The attributes that He prizes most are purity and love, and these are possessed only by the Christian."	The principle that God's impartial love impacts racial and ethnic variety is something that only the Christian can model. Tolerance, though popular in secular diversity, is not an option in Christian race relations. Cross-cultural love is the Christian's privilege. 1 John 4:7-12; 1 Corinthians 13.
"Those who have a religious experience that opens their hearts to Jesus will not cherish pride, but will feel that they are under obligation to God to be missionaries as was Jesus. They will seek to save that which was lost. They will not, in Pharisaical pride and haughtiness, withdraw themselves from any class of humanity, but will feel with the apostle Paul, 'I am a debtor both to the Greek, and the barbarians.'"	The principle of Christian missionary responsibility to the outcast and the less fortunate moves us beyond our homogenous communities. We minister to all because we owe all a debt of service. Romans 1:14.
"I know that that which I now speak will bring me into conflict. This I do not covet, for the conflict has seemed to be continuous of late years; but I do not mean to live a coward or die a coward, leaving my work undone."	The principle of Christian courage applies to race relations. It requires courage to love and serve "them" as God loves and serves "us." 2 Timothy 1:7.
"Jesus the Master was poor, and He sympathizes with the poor, the discarded, the oppressed, and declares that every insult shown to them is as if shown to Himself."	The act of incarnation means that Christ identifies with the poor and the marginalized. In fact, insults (racial slurs, racial epithets, and race-based jokes) offend Christ. Matthew 25:40.
"Those who have spoken harshly to them [Colored members] or have despised them have despised the purchase of the blood of Christ, and they need the grace of Christ in their own hearts."	Kindness to the vulnerable "least" among us is, in fact, kindness to Christ. Matthew 25:40.
"The God of the White man is the God of the Black man, and the Lord declares that His love for the least of His children exceeds that of a mother for her beloved child."	The historicity of the Creation narrative unites the various races into one family of interdependence. Acts 17:26.
"The Lord's eye is upon all His creatures; he loves them all, and makes no difference between White and Black,	The biblical truth is that social inequality attracts God's attention on behalf of the oppressed. Isaiah 58:4-9.

(Chart continued on next page)

110

except that He has a special, tender pity for those who are called to bear a greater burden than others."	
"The Black man's name is written in the book of life beside the White man's. All are one in Christ. Birth, station, nationality, or color cannot elevate or degrade men. The character makes the man. If a Red man, a Chinaman, or an African gives his heart to God, in obedience and faith, Jesus loves him none the less for his color. The day is coming when the kings of the earth would be glad to exchange places with the humblest African who has laid hold on the hope of the gospel."	We must reject the social doctrine of biological inferiority and affirm both biological and spiritual equality. Race as a basis of value is a social construct, a fallen invention of humankind. Galatians 3:27, 28.
"Those who slight a brother because of his color are slighting Christ."	Christ supports and identifies with the outcast. Acts 10:34-48.

Our Challenge

Ellen White knew that racial harmony is a matter of both the head and the heart. She contradicted popular scientific notions in her sermon by appealing to Scripture as the authoritative source for handling relationships between races. The principles that she applied to the Seventh-day Adventist Church of the nineteenth century are the same timeless principles that must be applied to the North American Division as it serves in the twenty-first century. Mrs. White made it clear in her sermon that she rejected the conclusions of the "social science" of her day. Clearly, racial differences did not denote inferiority or superiority, but opportunities for witness, service, and love.

In the twenty-first century, the Seventh-day Adventist Church faces the wonderful challenge of organizing its mission and fellowship around the same principles that actuated Ellen White. Practical questions for which we will find answers include: How will ethnic groups (i.e., Anglo, Asian, Latino, African, etc.) balance the need for same-race particularity in mission with the biblical mandate to be cross-cultural in our outreach (Matt. 28:18-20)? Will spiritual gifts be primary or subordinated to ethnicity in making pastoral assignments? How much diversity of structure will be acceptable, and how will the effectiveness of structural diversity be measured? The answers to these and other questions will require courageous leadership in the new millennium. Continued dialogue will expose how the ministry of Christ can create a culture of service, mission, and mutuality between the various racial and ethnic groups we call the Seventh-day Adventist Church.

[1] Andrew Hacker observes: "Since Europeans first embarked on explorations, they have been bemused by the 'savages' they encountered in new lands. In almost all cases, these primitive peoples were seen as inferior to those who 'discovered' them" (*Two Nations: Black and White, Separate, Hostile, Unequal* [New York: Ballantine Books, 1992], p. 26).

[2] However, it should be noted that in the nineteenth century there was a slowly developing consensus as to how many races existed. Attempts to identify racial groupings ran as low as Georges Cuvier's three and as high as Samuel Morton's 22.

[3] Chancellor William Harper, *A Memoir on Slavery* (Charleston, S.C.: Walter and Burke Printers, 1845), Microfiche, p. 5.

[4] Cited by John Hope Franklin, *Race and History* (Baton Rouge, La.: Louisiana State University Press, n.d.), p. 335.

[5] Cited by George Fredrickson, *The Black Image in the White Mind: The Debate on Afro-American Character and Destiny, 1817-1914* (New York: Harper and Row, 1971), pp. 63, 64.

[6] Cited by Harry V. Jaffa, *Crisis of the House Divided* (Chicago: University of Chicago Press, 1959), p 32.

[7] Thomas H. Huxley, *Lay Sermons, Addresses and Reviews—Emancipation: Black and White* (London: Macmillan and Co., 1895), p. 17.

[8] Nineteenth-century ideas on race illustrate how pervasive miseducation can be. So powerful was racist ideology that it took the collective resistance of a Civil War, three amendments to the Constitution, and a Civil Rights movement 100 years later to correct it.

[9] Louis B. Reynolds, *We Have Tomorrow* (Washington D.C.: Review and Herald Pub. Assn., 1984), pp. 19-22.

[10] Eugene Genovese, *Roll Jordan Roll: The World Slaves Made* (New York: Vintage Press, 1972), p 5; see also Genovese, *The World Slaveholders Made* (Middletown, Conn.: Wesleyan University Press, n.d.), pp. 98, 99.

[11] For a discussion on how inspired writers have related to the fallen institution of slavery, read Leslie Pollard,"Twentieth-Century Slavery," in *Message* magazine, Jan.-Feb. 1994, pp. 28, 29.

Chapter 12

FOUR STEPS FOR INTERCULTURAL ENGAGEMENT COMPETENCIES: A BIBLICAL MODEL

By Johnny Ramírez, Ed.D.

Professor of Religion, Loma Linda University

This chapter is based on psychological principles designed by God and modified by sin since the time of Adam and Eve. Only because God made us thinking entities is it important to understand how to develop competencies that we may not currently have. In further developing our minds, in moving in a positive way toward gaining the "mind of Christ" (1 Cor. 2:16), we can become more useful leaders of God's church.

The Creation and Flood stories make it clear that all humans were, are, and will be (until the second advent of Christ) under the corroding influence of sin. Therefore, all cultures share the same sinful background, all cultures need the redeeming power of the cross. No perfect culture and no perfect cultural set of values exists; from the people of Bible times to the present time, there was not, is not, and will not be a perfect culture that reflects all the values of Christ our Saviour.

True Christians will always acknowledge their shortcomings and their need of salvation and forgiveness: "Those who are really seeking to perfect Christian character will never indulge the thought that they are sinless."[1] Anyone who denies his or her sinful nature is fooling no one but himself or herself.

Considering current demographics, it is probable that the twenty-first century in America (as in many other countries) will be an age of intercultural relations, an age when there will no longer be a predominant majority group, when instead, all groups will represent less than 50 percent of the population and will need to coexist with each other. The age of the "world village" will arrive, when nations will be interconnected economically within an interdependent web. Can we afford to be closed-minded and ethnocentric in such an age?

Ethnocentrism, Racism, Prejudice, Stereotyping, and Bias Are Sins

Ethnocentrism is defined as "the practice of regarding one's own race or culture as superior to others."[2] This understanding is the root of all the other forms of "putting people down"—racism, prejudice, stereotyping, bias, disparaging persons who are not members of our cultural or racial group.

Love to God is truly defined only in the context of love for others. Those who assume that they can love God and hate or ignore their neighbors are lying to themselves and practicing a Christless Christianity. No one who hates or ignores his or her neighbor can fit the definition of being redeemed by Jesus. This is so because "whoever loves God *must* also love his brother" (1 John 4:21, NIV). Failing to love others and desire for them any less than we would want for ourselves falls short of gospel expectations.

Treating others according to a standard lower than the one by which we ourselves would expect to be treated has long been a pervasive human practice. Even after receiving the downpouring of the Holy Spirit, the apostolic age church members remained subject to ethnocentrism and the problems this sin causes (see Acts 10).

The New Testament and Today's Church

During the apostolic age of the Christian church we encounter manifestations of ethnocentric engagement, as registered in Acts 6:1-7. Seemingly, a few days after the early church received the gift of the Holy Spirit (Acts 2:1-47), tensions arose between the Hebraic Christian Jews and the Grecian Christian Jews. In other words, not even the presence of the Comforter was able to prevent the onset of intercultural tensions between different ethnic groups in the Christian church community.

The Seventh-day Adventist world church and its academic institutions, conferences, unions, divisions, hospitals, and publications are dependent for their day-to-day operation on people from all races, ethnic groups, and nationalities working together in harmony. Still, from time to time it becomes obvious that tensions arise from these intercultural relations. It therefore becomes imperative that we develop skills that will empower us to communicate effectively and engage successfully in productive cooperation across ethnic, race, and cultural boundaries.

Developmental Principle

It is a biblical New Testament concept that God blesses human efforts to develop our talents. In the parable of the talents (Matt. 25:14-30) Jesus introduced the stewardship concept of one's responsibility to develop the talents he or she has. The servants in the parable were expected to develop and use their talents; allowing them to remain undeveloped was not an option.

In the context of human behavior, psychologists and philosophers have discovered that humans' moral and cognitive abilities and competencies develop across time as they become increasingly proficient in the skills they favor and practice. As presented by psychologists Fischer, Hand, and Russell, human development takes place one skill at a time.[3] Therefore, developing the "mind of Christ" is a life process that takes place one skill at a time.

In this light, it is crucial for church leaders and members at large of the twenty-first-century North American and world church to develop the talents required for initiating successful intercultural engagements. Simply stated, leaders either develop these intercultural engagement talents or become obsolete and useless.

Developing Positive Intercultural Engagement Competencies

The development of intercultural engagement competencies may be categorized into a hierarchical order of four steps based on the logical complexity and developmental sequence for human cognition. We develop moral reasoning from the more simple logic of a 1-year-old child learning not to hit his newborn sister to the very complex logic involved in affirming the right of our adolescent daughter to reject our values while still loving her as if she were our very own image (which is no less than God does with us every day!). The individual who always gets things his or her way as a 1-year-old child, as an adolescent, and as a young adult will not be able to suddenly become a fair-minded adult. We develop morality via small steps that build on each other.

By adulthood humans have developed self-identity, including a cultural/ethnic identity. Although the acquisition of one's cultural/ethnic identity begins at an early age, most of its complex moral and ethical implications are not set until the adolescent years. Two factors contribute actively to this developmental process: (1) genetic/biological predisposition, and (2) environmental/cultural nurture.[4] Development of an ethnic identity is a cognitive task that all individuals accomplish, but many never realize they have since, as with many mental tasks, establishing ethnic identity can be a subconscious action. This means that although you may not be aware that you have an ethnic identity, you have one.

Following is a four-step model for understanding and promoting the development of such effective daily engagements under the guidance of the Holy Ghost:

Step 1: Personal cultural awareness. Many individuals believe that the notions shared by their community are universal norms that may vary according to individual interpretations, but are generally universally accepted as normative and binding. This is called ethnocentrism. Americans (or any other world citizen) who fail to realize that their heritage derives from a particular ethnicity (or mix of ethnicities) will be handicapped in moving away from ethnocentrism. They will perceive "being American" as being devoid of cultural ties, and will understand their way as the American norm coming from the "blank slate" of American heritage. Because of statistical, political, and economic historical realities, when individuals perceive themselves as merely Americans, with no other cultural ties, this invariably results in adopting the European-American mind-set.

The first step in the intercultural communication sequence is to acknowledge that each individual, as well as the prevalent cultural way (in America it is the European-American ways), has ethnic roots. This logical conclusion comes after recognizing that there are prevalent societal ways (followed by the majority) as well as discrepant social ways (followed by minority groups), an acknowledgment that results from generalizations derived from the data observed. After acknowledging their cultural/ethnic roots, individuals are capable of developing a desire to learn more about those roots. This worldview empowers individual self-examination and the recognition that being biased is a possible consequence of favoring one's unique way of doing things.

Step 2: Recognition of one's ethnic group and personal biases. Cultural thinking, as well as all other thinking, is learned by making generalizations: "No two circumstances are ever exactly the same, thus, intelligent beings constantly have to ignore differences and highlight similarities if they are to use their knowledge in new situations. The kind of analogizing that takes place in culture learning, however, is different from that which occurs, for example, in simple generalization."[5] In this cognitive way of learning culture by "analogizing," humans tend to generalize and stereotype others when deviations are found from what is conceived as the "normal" way of doing things. These generalizations are called biases and are an inseparable part of the human experience of intercultural communication.

The second step of the intercultural communication developmental sequence thus involves the recognition of cultural biases and stereotypes regarding other groups, and the perception of all cultural groups as being intrinsically equal. Individuals accept the fact that their preferred ways of conceiving social interactions and rules of behavior are, by definition, particular and not "normative," and that there is no such thing as "my way" being the proper or best way. Dealing with biases, this competency recognizes, is accomplished, not by ignoring them or pretending that legal codes or policy statements (as good and necessary as they may be) will cause their eradication, but by empowering individuals to acknowledge biases and deal with them as they inform personal and institutional interactions.

Step 3: Acceptance of other cultural perspectives as equal to one's own. This step is defined by the development of an openness toward, and a desire to learn more about, other cultural heritages, an attitude that comes from being able to work from more than one system of deductions, more than one cultural set of norms. Following a deductive approach from the previous step, that of recognizing one's ethnic group and one's own personal biases, leads to the need to accept other cultural perspectives as equally valid to one's own group's perspectives.

Note that each preferred way of doing things comes with a given set of biases against all other groups' preferred ways of doing things; this is because of the way things are conceived, not the way things are. Realization of this fact leads to the next logical conclusion, that one set of preferred ways cannot be universally better than all other sets of preferred ways, but are conceived that way only when compared to different ways of doing things. Thus individuals taking this step are empowered to examine and learn particular ways that are different from their group's way of doing things for the purpose of deliberately encompassing new cultural schemes into their cultural norms.

Included in this competency is a willingness to recognize discrimination by creating environments that empower minority groups within institutional and social settings, and a willingness to accept as legitimate viewpoints that are not fully understood. This is accompanied by a determination to risk self-vulnerability by direct participation in interactions under the control of other cultural groups.

Step 4: Active engagement in intercultural relationships. While differences and biases are natural parts of relationships, there is satisfaction in establishing permanent intercultural relations, including the desire to share leadership positions and power with all cultural ethnic groups that make up the church community, and by welcoming new groups into the faith community. The desire to overcome the fear of interacting socially within unfamiliar cultural contexts, of other ways of doing things, is hereby fostered and nourished as a moral imperative.

This competency promotes meaningful intercultural permanent relations, opening up the possibility of engaging in such relations for the sole purpose of enjoying communication with humans from different cultural heritages, as well as learning new ways of perceiving "reality." At this level, the possibility of incorporating new ways and ideas for the sole purpose of enjoying diversity, rather than for utilitarian purposes, is promoted. All human beings are capable of learning new ways, but those who have this competency are capable of perceiving this experience as pleasurable.

Conclusion

Each of these steps represents a particular competency. Acquisition of those competencies requires practice as well as a particular cultural environment that promotes or demands their development. These four steps represent the journey from an ethnocentric worldview to a better rounded version that allows, promotes, and enjoys diversity.

Four Intercultural Engagement Competencies for Church Leadership
(Sample Application to Church Worship Leadership)

Step 1: Self-awareness. The capacity to understand that the music style you prefer belongs to your cultural ethnic group (however this cultural group is defined, with as many influences as it may have), and that there is no knowledge of "heavenly" music outside our own preferences that were informed by our culture.

Step 2: Tolerance. The capacity to accept that your category of "sacred" music is as valid as the younger generation or the other cultural and ethnic group's categories of "sacred." This competency will tolerate diversity without exploring, enjoying, or accepting the validity of diversity.

Step 3: Reaching out. The church leader is now capable of exploring and beginning to enjoy diversity. In the sacred music example, this competency empowers the leader to promote a schedule of music for the church that represents the variety of definitions of "sacredness" that exist within the membership.

Step 4: Permanent engagement. At the highest level of development, the church leader is actively reaching out and establishing permanent bonds across cultural and ethnic boundaries. In the music example, the leader is enjoying the diversity of music styles while still preferring a particular style. This leader is now empowered to enjoy and promote diversity as part of a lifestyle that defines successful twenty-first-century leaders.

Great possibilities and opportunities are presented to a church leader who masters all four intercultural competencies; disappointment and frustration await leaders who lack these competencies. Develop intercultural engagement competencies as a way to "love your neighbor as yourself," or remain ethnocentric and egotistic, hiding your intercultural talents in the ground—this decision we as leaders face is deeply personal, but the benefits impact the whole church. Conflict and tension will be part of the process, but as the competencies are learned, solutions will come easier. Sin is a permanent human condition, and grace is a permanent divine intervention.

---

[1] Ellen G. White, *The Sanctified Life,* p. 7.

[2] *WorldBook Dictionary,* CD (Chicago, Ill.: 1999).

[3] Kurt W. Fischer, H. Hand, and S. Russell, "The Development of Abstractions in Adolescence and Adulthood," in M. L. Commons, F. A. Richards, and C. Armon, eds., *Beyond Formal Operations: Late Adolescent and Adult Cognitive Development* (New York: Praeger, 1984), pp. 43-73.

[4] R. F. Baumeister, *Identity: Cultural Change and the Struggle for Self* (New York: Oxford Press, 1986); Richard H. Dana, "Training for Professional Psychology: Science, Practice, and Identity," *Professional Psychology: Research and Practice* 18 (1987): 9-16; G. DeVos, "National Character," in D. L. Sills, ed., *International Encyclopedia of the Social Sciences* (New York: Macmillan and Free Press, 1968), vol. 11, pp. 14-19; E. E. Sampson, "The Decentralization of Identity: Toward a Revised Concept of Personal and Social Order," *American Psychologist* 40 (1985): 1203-1211; "The Debate on Individualism: Indigenous Psychologies of the Individual and Their Role in Personal and Societal Functioning," *American Psychologist* 43 (1988): 15-22; H. Triandis, "The Self and Social Behavior in Differing Cultural Contexts," *Psychology Review* 96 (1989): 506-520; H. Triandis et al., *Handbook of Cross-Cultural Psychology* (Boston: Allyn and Bacon, 1980), vols. 1-6.

[5] Claudia Strauss and Naomi Quinn, "Preliminaries to a Theory of Culture Acquisition," in Herbert L. Pick, Jr., Paulus Van Den Broek, and David C. Knill, eds., *Cognition: Conceptual and Methodological Issues* (Washington, D.C.: American Psychological Assn.,1992), p. 272.

Chapter 13

ASSESSING LEADER EFFECTIVENESS IN A DIVERSE WORLD

By Prudence LaBeach Pollard, Ph.D.

Associate Professor of Management
La Sierra University

This chapter is written with certain assumptions in mind:
- Effective leadership requires "followership."
- Diversity impacts leadership effectiveness.
- Leaders and followers must surmount cultural barriers.
- Not all cultures believe that formal assessment by a public is a good thing.
- Assessment, formal or informal, is a critical part of the personal improvement process.
- The more "objective" the data, the more quantitative, does not mean that the more precise will be the assessment of human competencies and characteristics.
- The more vested the individual is in the need for assessment data, the greater the likelihood that the individual will accept responsibility for self-development.
- Culture impacts the need for, types of, and processes for assessment of leader effectiveness.

Leadership styles are as varied as the people chosen to lead. Historically, we have done a good job with hindsight vision by declaring effectiveness after the eulogy has been read and the leader no longer has the opportunity to "mess up" our pronouncement. Today the situation is different as organizations seek ways to determine the effectiveness of their leaders. Reasons for this need arise from the desire to make objective personnel decisions to retain, promote, or terminate. The major question for those who study leadership remains: How can knowledge about leadership be used for training, and development? Most organizations that have good selection procedures are using leadership assessment to aid in the development of their valued leaders.

The earliest biblical record of this type of executive assessment approach to leadership development is recorded in Daniel 1. Nebuchadnezzar, king of Babylon, requested the selection and development of the best that Israel had to offer: young men, without defect, handsome, high aptitude for learning, well informed, quick to understand (keen intellect). The three-year development program consisted of dietary modifications and a curriculum to develop a strong cultural understanding of Babylon through the study of its language and literature, thus equipping them to serve in the king's palace. Daniel, one of the chosen young men, refused to defile himself with the royal food and wine, and requested a simple diet of vegetables and water. After the 10-day trial, Daniel's appearance was compared to those on the royal diet. The results were that Daniel looked healthier and better nourished than any of the subjects in the royal diet group, resulting in all of the young men being placed on Daniel's diet of vegetables. We see two things here:

1. Leadership selection and development is a strategic process; it should not be left to chance.

2. Leadership development should be assessed to identify the best way to obtain the desired outcomes.

Many studies have identified the skills needed for leaders to become and remain effective. Some have even summarized them into technical, interpersonal, and conceptual skills. When we move beyond looking at skills, personalities, and traits and move toward effectiveness, we will transition to results. An effective leader has an effect or impact on people, processes, and outcomes. Leadership assessments require the examination of these results.

A leader's effectiveness cannot be limited to measures of group productivity or satisfaction, although productivity and satisfaction are desirable outcomes of a leader's influence efforts. When we measure productivity or satisfaction, what assurance do we have that the leader was the primary cause of the improvement? This question implies that there are other indices for productivity and satisfaction. Leadership assessment, then, is not synonymous with organizational assessment. Leadership assessment is one of many components of an organizational assessment. We can ask those followers around the leader to tell of the impact of the leader's behavior on their own behaviors. However, for the leader who has a diverse following, asking is easier said than done (see Table 1).

When granted anonymity, Americans are candid in their views of their leaders. Other cultures are less open with their views. For example, it is unlikely that the Asian worker who views success as a collective effort will identify one person, the leader, as being solely responsible for the organization's success.

Table 1. Perspectives of Selected Countries[1]

COUNTRY	PERSPECTIVE
U.S.A.	• Data/practice orientation. • Quantification and measurement are useful and important. • Instrument-based assessment is popular. • Leading is learning by doing and practice.
France and Germany	• Observation/reflective orientation. • Reflection and theory are primary. • Leading is learning by intellect. • Facts/data in isolation can be seen as inferior thinking and dismissed as trivial.
Japan and China	• Greater appreciation for relational, synchronic, and metaphorical thinking rather than isolated, linear, analytical data. • Emphasizes the broader context of human relationships, family, to provide life's meaning. Individual has meaning within the context of relationships in organization, family, etc.

Keys to Effectiveness With Diverse Groups

To be considered effective by my own cultural group, I must deliver the leadership behavior valued by my group. It is no different for cultural groups other than my own; I must deliver the behaviors and results that are valued by that group. This requires knowledge of the leadership values of that culture. The following are five keys to effectiveness with diverse groups:

1. Recognize that cultural values shape expectations. Cultural values shape my leadership practices and affect how I assess its impact and how I want it assessed (see Table 2). Do I have a group-oriented view that leadership arises out of the efforts of the collective? Or do I have an individualist, egalitarian view that leaders have unique personalities and abilities that allow them to impact lives. Problems can arise when there is vast disparity between leader beliefs and followers' expectations. In those occasions, which are rapidly becoming the norm in our diverse, multinational organizations, we ought not make assumptions that the leadership perspective of the leader matches that of followers. For example, a leader with an individualistic view would be challenged to lead those with a collectivistic perspective, and vice versa.

Table 2. Cultural Value Orientations That Impact Assessments[2]

Cultural Values	Core Concepts	Countries at Ends of Continuum	Assessment Implications
Individualism versus collectivism. Independence versus interdependence.	Individual or self-responsibility versus group or organizational responsibility. Existential equality among people and emphasis on hard work and career versus preferential (religion, tribal membership, family ties, or friendships) treatment is natural.	U.S.A. versus China.	Effectiveness is individual's responsibility versus responsibility of the group. Authority through position; authority through seniority. Acceptance of assessment process is increased when directives come to individuals from those in authority; whereas group-oriented cultures respond more readily to assessment of the group and not of individuals within the group.
High context versus low context.	High use of nonverbal communication versus low use. Words receive special meanings in each context versus context less important to meanings. Relationship versus idea transmission.	Asia and South America versus U.S.A.	Meanings are conveyed by verbal and nonverbal means, therefore, written assessments may not capture the rich context. Scenarios must be clearly described because they affect the meanings of words used.
High power versus low power	Elitism versus egalitarianism. Conformity versus independence. Mistrust versus trust. Authoritarian versus census.	South America versus U.S.A.	Many organizational layers require more time and effort for supervisor buy-in. Directive from the top ensures participation versus group involvement needed for buy-in.
Ambiguity, tolerant versus certitude.	Pyramid versus flat organizational structure. Tolerance versus intolerance.		Assessment leads to change that is good versus change that is bad or unnecessary.
Open versus closed.	Open and responsive to change versus closed and less responsive.		Assessment policies needed versus policies not needed to encourage assessment.

(Table continues on next page)

123

Cultural Values	Core Concepts	Countries at Ends of Continuum	Assessment Implications
	Few written rules versus volumes of written policies.		
	Flexible versus inflexible.		
	People-orientation versus task-orientation.		
	Strategy-oriented versus detail-oriented.		
	Generalists versus specialists.		

Consider, for example, the General Conference of Seventh-day Adventists, a multinational religious corporation with a diverse group of leaders who represent and guide diverse cultures. The General Conference, with operations in Europe, the Caribbean, the Americas, Africa, and Asia, is no less diverse than Fortune 500 corporations with operations in Eastern Europe, South America, the Pacific Rim, and the United States. Both must successfully navigate within host cultures to effectively accomplish the mission of the organization. Additionally, at the General Conference headquarters we observe representatives from the various cultures searching for ways, sometimes foreign to their home culture, to work together. Therefore, to lead a diverse community, effective leaders will recognize their own cultural mind-set and study that of their superiors, peers, and followers so that knowledge of culture becomes a vehicle to increase the leader's effectiveness.

Authoritarian cultures value leaders who harness the authority of their positions and provide vision and direction that result in improvements in organizational life processes or returns on investment or quality of work life. In contrast, consensus-oriented cultures value leaders who treat the team as a unit, and develop ways to increase their cohesion and focus. *Leaders are valued and thereby deemed effective when followers' expectations are satisfied.* When assessing the effectiveness of leaders, we jeopardize the usefulness of the results when we do not account for the influence of follower culture on group expectations and processes.

2. Identify network of relationships. A leader's job is first to get things done through others, whether they are subordinates, peers, or consultants. Yet many organizations still depend solely on a superior's assessment to judge and reward performance. But we know that leaders spend most of their time with subordinates and the remaining time between superiors, peers, and others. This tells us that leaders deal with diverse groups, not just with superiors. Since leaders interact with *diverse* groups, then those groups are best able to provide developmental feedback to the leader. What are the leader's communication skills like? Or what is his or her ability to plan, delegate, require accountability like? For the leader who deals with organizational outsiders, such as suppliers or consultants, then those groups are also within the network of relationships.

3. Verify the expectations of the group. Identifying the expectations of followers is neither simple nor easy. It is even more challenging when the followers represent a diverse collage of cultures, races, languages, and so on. While this rich mixture provides opportunities to reflect the external environment; it also represents challenges. We can never assume that all peoples think alike.

We can illustrate this best with the contrast between Japanese and American societies. Ouchi relates the story of the Japanese workers who refused to participate in a company suggestion box program because of their belief that no one person can identify or solve a problem. Their cultural approach to tasks prevented any one person from attempting to identify a problem, much less recommend a solution. The philosophy was that when you work together, not in isolation, then the group, and not an individual, must share credit for any improvement. After changing to a group suggestion system, suggestions came pouring in.[3]

Add to that the American who tried to introduce a performance assessment program into a Japanese factory—he was rebuffed by Japanese workers, who saw this as criticism or praise of individuals and not the group, especially when it is the group that does the work.

4. Use assessments that are culturally appropriate. Select assessment methods that can get divergent groups involved in evaluating the impact of the leader's behaviors. Employing 360-degree feedback, i.e. feedback from peers, supervisors, and subordinates, requires the use of multiple raters to present a fair picture of a leader's effectiveness. This type of assessment allows leaders to listen to many groups. Here we have an excellent leader development opportunity. Managers can use the feedback to plan their professional development activities. A 360-degree view of the leader provides opportunities to reflect diversity at many levels (see Table 4):

- The instruments should reflect the values, communication styles, language, and workplace perspectives of the group. Because we have different expectations, we must listen to each group when developing our assessment instrument and reflect their values in the instruments; and for example, translate the instrument into the native language and then translate it back to assess whether the intended meanings are being communicated.
- The instruments should be formatted and administered in culturally sensitive ways. Americans are enamored with the idea of measurement—we measure everything, and so we give credence to the phrase, "Everything that is valued is measured, and everything that gets measured is valued." Other cultures ascribe value using other methods or may view counting as taboo. For example: for cultures that place high value on relationships, face-to-face interviews might be appropriate; for cultures that use many words and multiple word meanings to convey an idea (high-context versus low-context cultures) a face-to-face or telephone/e-mail mode of communication may offer opportunities to capture the subtleties of the conversation.

  During my childhood I remember that my grandmother would not allow certain things, such as livestock or fruit on a tree, to be counted (measured) by pointing of a finger. When one method of counting is taboo or seen as a source of ill will, then another method for counting requires consideration. In other locales, counting may be taboo, and in those cases a value other than a number may need to be substituted.
- The interpretation and meanings given to the leader's levels and types of effectiveness should reflect the values, communication styles, language, and workplace behaviors that were considered when the instrument was developed.

5. *Customize assessment processes.* These opportunities to gather diverse perspectives of organizational communities will be missed if the assessment does not reflect the community and if the desire for feedback is not ascertained (see Table 4). Some cultures are so individually competitive that leaders distrust the intent of peer feedback, which they fear would be too subjective and might be another way to have themselves eliminated. Other cultures value subtlety of meanings. High-context cultures are characterized by subtlety, so feedback has to be subtle, indirect, and face-saving.

Table 4.
Guidelines for Assessing Cross-cultural Leader Effectiveness

GUIDELINE:	RATIONALE:
1. Identify perspective of instrument developer	1a. Stereotypes and biases should be explored and accounted for to prevent integration into instrument or misinterpretation of results.
2. Customize instrument to culture	2a. The instrument should reflect the language, diverse perspectives, and the understandings of those who will complete the assessment. Example: translate the instrument into the native language and then translate it back to assess whether the intended meanings are being communicated.
3. Triangulation of methods	3a. Triangulation or using more than one instrument increases the validity of the information by minimizing the incidence of misinterpretation. Example: focus group followed by survey, followed up by telephone interviews of a sample.
4. Culturally sensitive format and delivery	4a. Format and delivery should not introduce tension. For example: collectivist cultures may have difficulty directly inquiring into the success of the CEO; or the American definition of "delegation of duties" may be valued in the U.S., while in France, for example, it may be viewed as shirking one's responsibilities.
5. Interpret and present results from cultural perspective	5a. Meanings are culturally derived. Allow the culture to give meaning to the findings. For example: if the feedback is that the executive spends many hours in his office, this may be highly valued in an authoritarian culture; whereas a more relaxed culture may view long hours as a sign of inefficiency.

Usually, though, in these context-rich cultures, group members deliver subtle feedback or superiors provide the assessment during informal interactions with their direct reports. With this indirect and informal feedback, the need for formal feedback is not as great as in low-context cultures. However, the need for formalizing feedback increases as the organizations become more diverse and global.

Multirater assessments provide a 360-degree view of the effectiveness of leaders. Well-developed instruments include a component to assess expectations of those completing the instrument. Then they rate the extent to which they observe the expected leader behaviors. Organizations planning to implement a leadership assessment program should consider the following recommendations:

1. Do not assume that an assessment instrument has global appeal. This must be confirmed.

    a. Pilot test the instrument on a small sample.

    b. Convene a panel of nationals to determine the appropriateness and relevance of concepts.

    c. Consider the need for anonymity and confidentiality.

2. Gather statements from each culture represented and develop dimensions of leadership that reflect each culture's bias.

    a. What behaviors do effective leaders demonstrate?

    b. Is it display of the behaviors that create effectiveness, or is it the extent to which the behaviors are observed? For example: effective leaders delegate to a greater extent than those who are ineffective.

    c. Does a high score reflect effectiveness?

    d. What about a low score?

    e. Should the focus be on the disparity between "the extent to which the behaviors are expected" and "the extent to which they are observed"?

3. Develop contextually appropriate assessment processes that respect cultural preferences for authority, seniority, collegiality, etc.

    a. Who will direct the process? Will it be top-down?

    b. Will the process assess individuals or groups?

    c. How will feedback be given, and by whom? Will feedback be from an insider or outsider/consultant? Will a senior employee deliver the feedback or will it be a junior employee?

4. Interpret and present assessment feedback using culturally sensitive models.

    a. Ensure that those who interpret and present the feedback are knowledgeable of the facts and assumptions that created the instrument.

    b. Determine who owns the feedback data. Is this the property of the leader or of the organization?

5. Keep in mind that the goal is not assessment, but development. Assessment is merely a means to an end, so remain willing to vary assessment methods.

Assessment of effectiveness gives leaders valuable insights into their influence-building behaviors within their network of relationships. When that network is diverse, as most networks are, then the assessment must be capable of capturing the rich context of the relationship. Using multiple raters to get a 360-degree view of the leader is a proven method for determining leader effectiveness. The keys and recommendations in this chapter will increase the usefulness of and receptivity to assessment in cross-cultural contexts.

---

[1] Some concepts were adapted from Hofstede (1980), in C. D. McCauley, R. S. Moxley, and E. van Velsor, *Handbook of Leadership Development* (San Francisco: Jossey-Bass Publishers, 1998).

[2] Countries identified from Hofstede (1980), in *ibid*.

[3] W. Ouchi, *Theory Z: How American Business Can Meet the Japanese Challenge* (New York: Avon Books, 1981).

Additional reading:

Webber, R. *Culture and Management.* Homewood, Ill.: Richard D. Irwin, Inc., 1969.

SUCCESS SECRETS

of Effective DIVERSITY LEADERS

SECTION 2

INTERVIEW WITH ALVIN M. KIBBLE
President, Allegheny East Conference

Interviewer: Leslie N. Pollard, D. Min.

Vice President for Diversity
Loma Linda University Adventist Health Sciences Center

Pollard: How long have you been a worker in the church and in what capacities have you served?

Kibble: I am celebrating my thirty-first year in ministry. I began my ministry in August 1969. I have served as a camp pastor for our conference youth camp—Camp Monotoni, as it was called at that time. I have served as a pastor in several districts in our conference in the states of Maryland, New Jersey, and Virginia, and for the past 15 years I have been in church administration, serving as secretary of the Allegheny East Conference, then as vice president for ministerial affairs and director of church ministries, and since January of 1989 I have served as president. . . . Most recently I have been serving also as the chairperson for the North American Division Council of Regional Presidents and the Black Administrators' Caucus.

Pollard: And the . . . council represents a constituency of how many people?

Kibble: Just under 300,000.

Pollard: Tell me a little more about your definition of leadership.

Kibble: Well, I believe that, in fact, the essence of leadership, and of course, from a biblical perspective, would be to influence others for the kingdom of God or the kingdom of heaven. So in that sense we have a prescription and a commission that is given to us by God. The leadership models that I have observed from the Bible and which I cherish are those of shepherding, of mentoring, and of equipping. And each way it offers the opportunity to provide a certain quality of care and a sense of direction for a support group, whether it be the world, or whether it be the local church, or whether it is simply your family.

Pollard: **You have talked about leadership. Corporations today have taken diversity very seriously. You name one, and almost all of them have departments, directors, and vice presidents of diversity. Why do you think corporations have taken diversity so seriously?**

Kibble: Well, I think what is driving corporations is what Dr. Martin Luther King, Jr., said some years ago, "that we are all dressed in one garment of humanity." We are discovering the reality of that today more so than ever before. Steven Covey talks about the removal of the safety nets. There are no more safety nets in our society, and all of our problems are global in nature, whether we are talking about global warming, or whether we are talking about ecological problems, or whether we are talking about health problems, AIDS, cancer, whether we are talking about communications. The reality is that we will never complete the gospel commission by ourselves.

Pollard: **You talk about the commission; the commission to go into all the world is a global commission.**

Kibble: We were given this as a people, which, to me, says that Christ is not going to come any sooner to Black people or to the Allegheny East Conference than He is to the rest of the world, and the forces that threaten us and the challenges that we face are of such that no group is exempt, and therefore, what aids me may also aid and be of assistance to others. And what threatens me can equally be a threat to others.

Pollard: **I want to ask you a question that is a little more sensitive. There are people who believe that as a leader of the**

North America Division regional work you reach out only to people of African descent. What would you say to people who say regional conferences do not do diversity?

Kibble: For the record, the Black Seventh-day Adventist Church has always been integrated. It was integrated when I was a child growing up in Chicago, an urban city that was a melting pot; it was so then as it is today. Latinos were no strangers to Blacks, and neither were Asians or the Indians. They have been a part of our community as the Jewish people have been. The Black church is a microcosm of the Black community. That is just a fact of history. On the other hand the regional conferences have contributed greatly to the church as proper and effective models of ministry, and I think that is a concept that has not been fully studied and a contribution that has not been fully appreciated. When you look at the church, when you try to define what the church is, you have no better example than the Black SDA Church, which, out of necessity, had to create a sense of community for itself in its faith experience. Out of that grew the concern for our children, for our elderly, for our families. It became that safe haven, it became that voice of advocacy, it became that nurturing center.

Pollard: **One hundred million dollars is more than some divisions pay in tithe, isn't it?**

Kibble: It represents the largest tithe base outside of the North American Division itself. It is the second-largest tithe base, if you were to speak of it in those terms, outside of the North American Division itself. You should also know that the tithe that is contributed to the General Conference is equal to the amount of tithe that is appropriated by the General Conference to all the divisions of the world church.

Pollard: **What is the significance of that?**

Kibble: Well, it suggests at least that . . . the [tithe] appropriations that the church . . . in turn gives to the Black work around the world is more than sufficiently provided for by the nine regional conferences in their appropriations to the General Conference.

Pollard: **What about Allegheny East? How diversified is it?**

Kibble: We presently record some 27,000 members, of those we have approximately 1,500 who are Franco-Haitian; we have a growing . . . Hispanic membership, which may equal the membership of several of our sister conferences who have had a long history in the Spanish work. We have four Korean churches. We have an Indonesian church, we have a church of East Indians (who speak the Telagu language), that we have most recently organized, and we also have a West African church.

Pollard: **So is there special preparation that you do before talking to one of your multicultural groups?**

Kibble: I think that one of the critical needs, especially if you are working in a diversified setting, is that of awareness. I find it important to get to know something about the various cultures that we serve, and particularly the cultural imprints of these ethnic groups.

Pollard: **Now, how do you access that knowledge?**

Kibble: Much of it has to be through dialogue.

Pollard: **With the group?**

Kibble: With the group leaders. I don't want to make the mistake that the majority culture has made again and again with Black people of assuming that I am an expert on their culture.

Pollard: **So you let the group, then, teach you about themselves?**

Kibble: And rightly so. No culture is an open book, and the best way for us to become aware is to be teachable, to be willing to become students. Our finest educators today realize that that is the apogee of education. When we are all learners—and I

136

think that it is affirming, since leadership is the ability to influence—it is affirming when the particular culture or ethnic group understands and appreciates the fact that the leader knows what he or she does not know, but evidences a willingness to learn in order to more greatly serve. This is what Christ did for us in the Incarnation experience. He, perhaps of all leaders, . . . had the need to become man in order to understand man, but He knew that man needed the example and the relational contact that would ensure our confidence that He understands.

Pollard: **What other skills do you see leaders needing? You mentioned a kind of sensitive learning; what are the skills that you believe are necessary for multicultural leadership? Skills? Insights? Attitudes?**

Kibble: I think leadership begins with a genuine love for people.

Pollard: **Why do you say that?**

Kibble: Because if you are not a lover of people, you will not have the stamina or the patience that is needed in order to carry out the leadership task.

Pollard: **I like your words stamina and patience because that appears to be what cross-cultural leadership requires.**

Kibble: Cross-cultural leadership is more than just a job; it pushes the envelope beyond that. The human tendency is to set up limits on how far we will go in an effort to understand an issue before trying to resolve it. But your love for the people enables you to go the extra mile. And then you develop a mutual respect that puts in place certain guarantees. . . . Respect cautions us against taking shortcuts as if we are dealing with inventory or dealing with figures, but when you are dealing with persons, it is going to ensure [a high] quality of leadership because you are dealing with individuals as persons rather than as statistics or as social classes, [with people's] self-esteem. I don't think that this is a role for individuals who are still struggling to find out who they are.

Pollard: **How are leaders benefited by cultural self-knowledge?**

Kibble: Having a high sense of self-esteem and knowing who you are positions you to be more vulnerable as you interact with others, and for me, like love, leadership has to be vulnerable. You are putting yourself out in front where your mistakes are easily seen by others, where people can and will question and critique your behavior, your attitude, your assumptions.

Pollard: **What else is needed for effective multicultural leadership?**

Kibble: Flexibility. Willingness to change . . . your view of things, to change your perceptions, your prejudices, and we all have them. I think that any time you are dealing in a cross-cultural ministry you have to [be] open for change, because, [as] I said earlier, we all have our own imprint. Growing up, as I did, in an urban community, and for the first 10 years of my life attending an urban church school and junior academy, it was somewhat of a cultural challenge for me when in the eleventh grade I transferred to the Illinois Conference boarding academy, Broadview. Not only did it introduce me more consciously to my own cultural imprint, but it helped to identify the differences that others had in relationships, the things that I kind of took for granted and related to in a natural and kind of automatic knee-jerk response.

Pollard: **As Adventists, we have not been known for participating in justice ministry. As a representative of the Black Seventh-day Adventist Church, do you see a basis for undertaking such a ministry?**

Kibble: Yes. If we would apply the values that we propose for religious liberty to social liberties, we would not even recognize ourselves.

Pollard: **Tell me about that; that is a unique observation. If we**

were to approach social liberty as we approach religious liberty, what would happen?

Kibble: We would catapult ourselves to the forefront of society as leaders and as exponents of what I believe is really the gospel commission. We would develop a very sharp and a very equitable approach toward the religious issues that would draw conflict and criticism; we would bocame exponents of religious freedom and lead the religious world. But because, at least in terms of the majority leadership of our church, we have not had the experience of seeing life from the [perspective of the] minority cultures, we have been totally oblivious to those issues and to the sensitive concerns that we should have and should maintain and be advocates for, given our Christocentric heritage.

Pollard: Now, on religious liberty I am going to see if we can apply this, and you tell me if this is true or false. If we had taken our religious liberty passion and applied that to the Civil Rights movement, where would we be today as an Adventist Church?

Kibble: We would have been the models for the world.

Pollard: And what did the marchers want during the Civil Rights movement? There are some that say we shouldn't get involved with political causes, but what did the people want?

Kibble: The people wanted desegregation, it was not so much integration as it was desegregation.

Pollard: What is the difference between the two?

Kibble: Desegregation removes the laws that prevent us from our inalienable rights: housing, quality education, safety, health service, employment, transportation. The privilege and the dignity that should be extended to every person. I can remember one of our pioneer Adventist couples who when they had to board a train, the husband had to separate from the wife because he was of Black pigmentation and she appeared White. What an insult to their human dignity. So these were the things that they were striving for?

Pollard: **When we think about the next generation of young people, what would we say to them now to get them ready to assist in readiness for multicultural leadership in this church and in the next century?**

Kibble: I think we have to begin with helping them to become whole persons and unapologetic for who they are. Whether Korean or Filipino or Japanese or Latino, whether Asian or Jamaican or Black American, we must help our children to find acceptance in who they are, and we need to create more and better opportunities where they can test their ethnicity in a forum of diversity where they can learn to uncover the true essence of humanity and Christianity, and learn to celebrate their Christianity without denying their ethnicity.

Pollard: **Thank you very much.**

INTERVIEW WITH MANUEL VASQUEZ, D.MIN.
Vice President for Multicultural Ministries
North American Division

Interviewer: Johnny Ramirez, Ed.D.

Professor of Religion
Loma Linda University

Ramirez: **Can you tell us a little bit about yourself; what characterizes you?**

Vasquez: I think of myself as a very positive, energetic person, someone who dedicates most of his time to the service of the church. I awaken thinking about . . . things I need to do at the office and for special projects that I am working on. After work at the office, I come home and do a little inventory of what I have done and try to line myself up mentally for the next day. I live for the church. I don't have any outstanding hobbies. My whole life is the church.

Ramirez: **How were intercultural relations at Manuel High School in Denver, Colorado, when you were a student there?**

Vasquez: When I was growing up, and especially in grade school through junior high, it was a period in our American history when minorities were really looked down on. We Hispanics had a lot of problems with other kids picking fights with us. There was not a sense of pride among Hispanics. Self-esteem was lacking. There were no historical figures in American history to look up to. We had no role models; I didn't know of any Hispanic lawyers or doctors or even teachers. I wasn't aware of any Hispanic leaders. Consequently, we were embarrassed and ashamed of our ethnicity. Intercultural matters at junior high were nil. I mean, Hispanics stuck together and never mingled with anybody else.

Ramirez: **What happened in the Navy that changed your life?**

Vasquez: Well, the Navy was a turning point in my life because that is where I came under the conviction of Adventist teachings. I was baptized while I was in the Navy and came under a strong conviction to turn my life around and do something for the Lord. So the Navy had a great impact on me. I witnessed a lot during my Navy tour, not always as a member, because I was baptized later. I had a lot of beautiful Christian experiences as a Seventh-day Adventist believer. Even before my baptism, I conducted myself as a member, abstaining from all the things our church teaches [us to abstain from].

Ramirez: **So what kind of model were you developing between your home, Manuel High School, [and] the Navy? When you went to college, what kind of model did you have in your mind of intercultural relations in America?**

Vasquez: Well, there were really no intercultural relationships. When I went to college, even though it was an Adventist college, the situation wasn't much different. In those days Hispanics kept kind of to themselves as well. The Anglo students didn't really involve us unless we spoke really good English. I felt disenfranchised all the way through school, and even somewhat the same in college.

Ramirez: **How did the presentation of the gospel impact the intercultural model? What was your dream of what heaven should be?**

Vasquez: The ideal that was always in my mind was that we are made of one blood. God is our Father, and we should see each other with respect, care, and love. I longed for that. I am not saying that I was mistreated at college; it is just that there was no real relationship, no commonality. There was no affinity among the races. We didn't have a whole lot in common with the Anglos so that we could be friends. I felt more comfortable with Hispanics, so we just mingled together.

Ramirez: **Do you see yourself as a mentor? Do you have some mentorees whom you are hoping to help in the process of becoming leaders in the work?**

Vasquez: Yes. Since that is a void in my life, I try to make myself available and freely give counsel to young Hispanics. I also take people under my wing. I've always seen myself as a father figure for the younger men; I'm like a father. For men who are more mature and closer to my age, I still give counsel, but more as a colleague. Whenever a Hispanic becomes a president or is promoted to a new position, I always write them a letter and give them pointers. I take my coordinators under my wing and try to mentor them to help them develop their leadership skills.

Ramirez: **Leadership today involves intercultural relations. Corporations outside of Christianity are paying lots of attention to Hispanics, Blacks, and other minorities. Do**

you think the church is doing the same? Do you see the Seventh-day Adventist Church in North America following this leadership?

Vasquez: Not at the same level, but it's getting there. The division does provide minimal subsidies for these groups, and some local fields have provided coordinators. Presently, I oversee 26 non-English language groups. In my leadership role over these different ethnic, non-English-language groups, I've learned also to be a leader for them, and to mentor them. I'm trying to help them grow as well. I do a lot of cross-cultural ministering with these members. However, initiatives that function, or work, for one group don't necessarily work in another group. I think our church could do a lot more. It could be more proactive in meeting the needs of the minority non-English-language groups.

Ramirez: **What would you advise the new wave of leaders who are perhaps now in college or in graduate school or in beginning positions and are growing up in leadership to do in order to prepare themselves to confront this reality in the church?**

Vasquez: All are leaders who are going to be in place for the new millennium [and] should get training in multi- and cross-culturalism. In a matter of just 12 to 15 years, for example, the Hispanics are going to be the largest ethnic minority group in the United States. The Koreans are coming in waves (Asians) and are very susceptible to the message. Russians are coming to America and need to be given the opportunity to hear the Advent message. Leaders would do well if they would learn a second language.

Ramirez: **You mentioned the need for cross-cultural and intercultural communication and leadership skills. Could you list some of the specific elements of those skills, or specific skills in particular, that leaders need to be developing?**

Vasquez: Besides the usual leadership skills, including computer technology, the new millennial leaders will, of necessity, need to develop a sensitivity and working skills to reach out and minister to the masses of ethnic minorities. As I mentioned before, some will want to acquire a second language. That, in itself, will give them a greater appreciation for multilingual ministry.

Ramirez: **Do you think that search committees throughout the denomination and throughout our institutions, colleges, and universities should list as one of their requirements for leadership "cross-cultural competencies," and perhaps include some [input] from underrepresented individuals [as to] qualifying characteristics for this leader to be considered?**

Vasquez: Yes, I think any leader who is being considered for a position . . . should be interviewed . . . by Hispanic leaders or African-American leaders whose lives he may be impacting. With a number of questions they can discover his or her attitude toward these minority groups. If he or she is open to them, if he or she is sensitive to them, if he or she looks down upon them, if he or she sees them as equals. Those who don't measure up should be disqualified from leadership roles that impact the greater number of constituencies in the divisions that have a multicultural constituency.

Ramirez: **Some of our groups, like African-Americans, do organize and discuss agenda items among themselves before going to boards and constituency meetings. And they usually come with a unified agenda and a unified voice so as to get the political power necessary to accomplish the goals that would benefit the church at large and that particular group. Do Hispanics do the same thing?**

Vasquez: Hispanics cannot do the same to the extent that the African-Americans do. They have conferences, presidents, and officers, and they do have a caucus that is recognized by the North American Division, which Hispanics don't have. However, the Hispanics periodically get together to discuss items that impact not only their work, but the work of the whole church.

144

Ramirez: Do you think there are some cultural values that meet that outlook, perhaps values of humility and some mission, or how do you explain this difference? Is it only statistics, or are there some cultural values that make us different from African-Americans?

Vasquez: Well, there are some cultural differences. Hispanics are not as activistic and are not as united. Hispanics cover the gamut from Caucasian to African and in between. Even Asians, Arabs, and Jewish, so not all the time are Hispanics visibly identified. Some are considered Anglo; some are considered Black. Since they are made up of many countries, 20 Hispanic countries, they are not always as united.

Ramirez: As you dream of the future of this church that you love and [for which] you have already given 31 years of hard labor of love, what kind of vision do you have for the intercultural relations of the church as the twenty-first century begins? Paint the picture for us.

Vasquez: The next millennium will be the millennium, especially in this division, of multiculturalism. If our church does not seriously address multicultural ministry, cross-cultural ministry, it is going to be left behind. Soon there will not be a majority of any one group in the country. The main church in North America will be more multicultural than multilingual. I see the future of our inner-city churches, English churches, and even some of the ethnic churches becoming multicultural rather than a single language or multilanguage. Even now some Spanish churches have Anglos, African-Americans, Portuguese—and even some Asians—attending. My own church, . . . the Washington, D.C., Spanish church on New Hampshire Avenue, has a bilingual service, with Anglos, African-Americans, Portuguese, and occasionally, Asians visiting there. It is a service of 80 to 120 young people. It is done bilingually. But I see this trend in California. California is a kind of a pacesetter for this kind of ministry. I see some English churches with many Hispanics, Asians, and Blacks worshiping with them, and they are losing that Caucasian flavor. It is becoming a multicultural ministry in these churches. I think this is where the future is. It is going to be a little bit of heaven, as heaven is going to be that way. And I see that as a model for the twenty-first century.

Ramirez: **What would you say to the female leader who is in the beginning stages of her leadership?**

Vasquez: I would tell a female leader aspiring to be a leader in this church, either in ministry or in administration, to take hold of Joel 2:28 and embrace that. I would say, "God, if You are going to use me to minister, so be it. But give me the direction and open doors for me." Women, stand tall and make yourselves available for service. I believe the greatest days for women in ministry and leadership are just ahead of us.

Ramirez: **Thank you, Elder Vasquez.**

INTERVIEW WITH MARDIAN BLAIR, CEO
Adventist Health Systems, Sunbelt

Interviewer: Benjamin Reaves, Ph.D.
Vice President for Ministries, Adventist Health Systems Sunbelt

Reaves: **You have been and are currently a worker in the church. In what capacities have you served?**

Blair: For one and a half years I was a staff accountant and development coordinator at Hinsdale. For three and a half years I was a vice president at Hinsdale. For the past 38-plus years, [I have been] a hospital/health system CEO.

Reaves: **What were your early days of leadership like?**

Blair: Well, as an accountant—actually, I was a billing clerk; accounting was a little glorification of the term—[I found it] a

146

very routine job, important in the sense that it had to be done, but I groaned a bit under that because I was well educated and trained well beyond that and thought my time would never come. As coordinator of development I worked with the leaders of Hinsdale who had an interest in the hospital, and that was usually an exciting experience. The assistant administrator role was tremendous too, because the administrator was in his years just before his retirement, and he was ready to turn things over to me. I was learning, and I worked more or less on an unlimited basis to get experience and get things done. I had a great time.

Reaves: **And when you say you had a great time, I would imagine that includes the fact that you were, as you indicated, learning about leadership and some of these people, some of whom you might have already referenced. Did they serve as mentors for you? Can you think and identify in your mind—**

Blair: The one mentor I had who was really an enormous mentor to me was . . . A. C. Larsen, the CEO at Hinsdale. He had been a hospital leader for 30 or 40 years. He was a great man. And then I worked very closely a few years later with Walt Blehm, who was president of the Oregon Conference—he was . . . a great leader in my opinion.

Reaves: **When you think of those mentors and try to identify some of the valued lessons that you picked up, . . . as far as the administrative skills and responsibilities or the matter of how to relate to people, what do you think you came away with? Or was it the matter of sometimes you've got to grit your teeth, hang in there, and get the job done, or was it all of the above?**

Blair: Well, you know what you learn, but it's really hard to pin [down] where you learned it. Particularly if you do a lot of reading, which I've done. I know I learned from this gentleman, Mr. Larsen. It was more about the church that I learned from him, the Adventist Church and the Adventist health work, because he would spend hours telling me stories and experiences, and they were 99 percent positive. He occasionally told me about some of the mistakes that have occurred in people's lives and in the life of the church, but I knew he was loyal and it didn't bother me. But it was really tremendous. The thing I probably learned most from him was integrity. He was flawless, and any shadow of irregularity would be the death knell in his mind. That made a very strong impression on me, but he was a highly competent leader, too. And I learned a lot from him in that regard.

Reaves: **Can you describe a time when as a leader you felt most challenged?**

Blair: There were two times. When I went to Portland, Oregon, to build the Portland Adventist Medical Center, the land was already bought, and I ran into an absolute firestorm there because it was to be built on a golf course and the Sierra Club and all kinds of groups were opposing it, and it was about a three-year nightmare. Court cases, large public hearings . . . with 1,000 people present, many of which were extremely angry, and to be speaking to them was really difficult, and you wondered whether you would ever make it. But after a while I got so I actually enjoyed it, and we accomplished our purpose after a while—not on that site—but a great site. That was a terrible experience in some ways, but a wonderful experience in other ways. And then when I came into the Adventist Health System, there was an extremely difficult financial problem—we didn't have any money, no cash, and the operations were running millions of dollars behind, and we thought we might run out of cash. I can't think of a more terrifying experience in business than being the chief executive officer and thinking you could, in fact, go bankrupt and have thousands of people affected by that bankruptcy. We never really got close to bankruptcy, but we got close to being in default, and that was a problem, and then building out of it . . . took several years of very intense work on the part of many people. Those were the only two, I guess you'd say, terrifying experiences of my business life.

Reaves: Let me shift our conversation a little bit. Corporations are now taking the matter of diversity very seriously, . . . do you have any thoughts on why this might be so, and what kind of implications does diversity have for church leadership?

Blair: I would presume that corporations, in general, are recognizing the importance of diversity for pure business reasons. In other words, there is a pool of talent that, if they get to that talent before somebody else does, [will put them] in better shape businesswise. That's probably what's driving business. That same reason would probably drive church business, but there're other issues at work as well.

Reaves: Would you feel, then, that the church's attentiveness to diversity [where] business or organizational benefit is included [might indicate that] there is also an undergirding conviction?

Blair: The church has a much more complex response to diversity—the church is made up of a diverse population, therefore, the church is representative—it must include its diverse membership. The facts are that church organizations like Adventist Health System need the best people from wherever we can get them. And so, even if we didn't have a responsibility to share leadership and the work of the Adventist Health System with diverse groups, we would be insane not to do it for purely business reasons.

Reaves: As far as the church is concerned—you are very active in church life—do you feel that there are opportunities for multicultural leadership in the church?

Blair: I think so. I'm not as expert on general church leadership as I am on health, but I see a world of difference today [compared to] when I started in the work of the church in the late 1950s. There are all kinds of people who are multicultural from different ethnic backgrounds in leadership compared to the past, and I think that's good. As long as a person is competent, I think they ought to, you know, roll. And if they're not competent, no matter what ethnic background they are, they shouldn't be in that job.

Reaves: **To carry out multicultural leadership, are there particular skills that . . . you feel would be necessary?**

Blair: There are skills for a CEO or other leader going into a multicultural setting, and then there's the issue of a person of a different ethnic background other than Caucasian going into leadership also. And I don't presume to be an expert on this, but a leader who is in a multicultural setting must be broad-minded and not have a chip on his or her shoulder against diverse cultures, because sooner or later that's going to show up. It will just rise to the surface at some crisis point, and he or she will say something that is demeaning to somebody or some group, and he or she will lose . . . credibility or . . . will treat people in a way that is, in comparison to Caucasian people, or White people, noticeably different. So I think there's got to be an inherent nonprejudicial attitude in his or her mind relating to other people. On the other hand, an ethnic person leading in a predominately White environment has got to have some pretty good skills in order to not make the same kind of mistakes. They are a little different, but if he or she employs people who shouldn't be employed because of their competency he or she will immediately create problems. As long as he or she employs people of all races who are competent, and treats people the same way I referenced earlier, it will work. But that is a very complex area—I don't presume to be an expert.

Reaves: **You are viewed as someone who has exhibited some of those skills in . . . leading across multicultural lines. Now, when you know that you are making a presentation before a multicultural group, is there any kind of special preparation or research that you do?**

Blair: Well, I hadn't quite thought of it as doing [anything special]. Any group that I would speak to, I try to assess who they are and be sure that I touch on things of interest to that group. And I would also avoid any hot buttons for any group, and there are certain words that are hot buttons, and I would never knowingly use anything that would offend a group. But you're speaking to them to communicate some thought and also to build goodwill, so anything you do that's contrary to that is a mistake.

Reaves: **Have you ever seen anybody blow it in a cross-cultural situation? Have you ever witnessed—**

Blair: I have witnessed that one time, and it was horrible. Clearly the person was a good person—a White man who was using slang that was clearly inappropriate, and in the days that he lived, it was not considered inappropriate in a White setting. When he used it, it created terrible problems.

Reaves: **Do you think that experience contributed to the sensitivity that a lot of people feel you have about people and relationships in a cross-cultural setting?**

Blair: It might; I don't know. You know, my wife and I were at the General Conference [session] in Holland, and there was a little lady with a very large suitcase there who didn't—a little Black lady from England, I think—know how to get to her hotel. She had this huge suitcase, monstrous suitcase, and totally helpless, maybe 70 years old, maybe in her sixties, I don't know, but she was in a problem. We took her from the GC, I think, downtown on the train and then by taxi to her hotel; [we] just took care of it, and I probably would do that for any person in need, but I think a Black person in a foreign nation is much more vulnerable than a White person, and so both my wife and I did that, and I think there's probably been a number of cases in my life where that incident in college probably impacted me. I'm not sure how much, but I think it has.

Reaves: **Do you recall any experiences over your career where you have had to address someone who was guilty of less-than-thoughtful sensitivity? Have you ever had to**

151

call someone's hand in a discreet way or in any way?

Blair: I have. Not many times, because in the Adventist Church I don't find many people who if they have racial feelings, they don't manifest it—not in this day and age. There have been a few times, not many.

Reaves: **And were you uncomfortable in calling it?**

Blair: Not really, you know it's . . . an injustice in any case.

Reaves: **So integrity comes back into the picture again?**

Blair: Yeah, I suppose.

Reaves: **As we talk about leadership in Adventist Health System and what the future holds for us, as we look at the church as it moves into the next millennium and the leadership demands for the church, is there something the AHS can do to prepare the next generation of leaders for effective multicultural leadership?**

Blair: There probably is . . . the issue of everybody being truly equal is something that I don't believe has fully sunk in everywhere. Now, I don't mean equal under law, or equal under God; I mean equal. My feeling and working premise is that a little Spanish kid who has ability and character . . . all they need is education and, through that process, the motivation—and that would apply to a Black child, Indian, or Oriental. . . . The same number of people of ability or lack of ability, percentage-wise, are in every population. Now, you find people who are motivated by their families and circumstances, and that probably varies somewhat. But the Adventist Health System needs to find these capable young people and incorporate them into its operations from whatever ethnic background they are, and we will prosper because of that, and have. I believe there is tremendous opportunity for young people today. I think in health care especially.

Reaves: As I indicated earlier on, you are seen as an effective cross-cultural leader. Are there any, again, skills that you might recommend to young people in order for them to exercise effective leadership in a multicultural world?

Blair: Yes, I think so. I think leaders, whatever their ethnic backgrounds are, and if they're White, they have to be more sensitive, need to see people as equal, as needing opportunities, and treat everybody equitably. Now, I find with doctors that a non-Adventist doctor in an Adventist hospital has to be treated just a bit better to feel equal. Because you go to church with the Adventist doctors, you go to school board meetings with them, prayer meetings, or whatever, and when you see them you greet them differently. See, there is a more close, warm greeting. Now, I believe that people of ethnic backgrounds have a sensitivity that they are not being treated fairly, and therefore you've got to do something a little extra at times to get them to feel that it is an equal playing field.

Reaves: That's an interesting observation, and what I think I hear you saying is that it may take more effort, or more proactive initiative, to bring a comfort level to people of, say, a minority background who are working in a majority situation.

Blair: That's absolutely correct. If I see a young lady or man who's ethnic, non-White, I try to be particularly friendly to that person because I know that they feel a little bit shorted, and I want them to feel good about the Adventist Health System.

Reaves: And you recognize that the perception for many people of Adventist Health System rides to some degree on their perception of you as leader. And if that is true, then for any kind of leadership responsibility there needs to be the awareness that perception of the organization, in many ways, rests with the image presented by the leader.

Blair: Of course, that applies, and I agree with that point, but that applies all across the board. You in your work at Oakwood College—people look at the college as a lengthened shadow of its leader. Now if you've been there only six months, it's a pretty short shadow, but if you've been there a long time, you do put an imprint on the organization, whether it's good or bad. And that has to do with racial relationships, it has to do with integrity, because people do what the leader does, and if the leader is questionable in his expense reporting, or no matter what he or she does, other people are going to sort of adopt that practice. If the leader works hard, the company works hard; if the leader is ethical, the company is ethical to a large extent, not perfectly. So leadership in racial relationships is very critical, but that applies across the board. There is just no substitute for effective leadership.

Reaves: **Thank you very much.**

INTERVIEW WITH CALVIN B ROCK, PH.D., D.MIN.
Vice President, General Conference

Interviewer: Leslie Pollard, D.Min.
Vice President for Diversity, Loma Linda University

Pollard: **I want to talk to you about leadership, but first I would like to ask you to share just with us a little bit about your background.**

Rock: I was born in New York City during the latter part of the Depression. My mother took us—my sister and me—to Los Angeles when I was 11. We were a one-parent family. We settled in Los Angeles; in fact, my mother still lives in southern California. At college age I went to Oakwood [College]. And even before that I spent a year at Pine Forge Academy in Pennsylvania. Since then I have been involved in life all over the country. Following Oakwood, I pastored in the South

Atlantic Conference for 12 years, then in the Lake Region Conference for four years, and then served three years in the Southern Union Ministerial Association. That was followed by a year and a half in the Northeastern Conference, pastoring again, and then 14 years of presidency at Oakwood College. Since 1985 I have been one of the general vice presidents of the General Conference. Between the beginning of my pastorate in Detroit and the conclusion of my work at Oakwood College, I spent a number of years in various universities earning graduate degrees that have provided me very helpful insights for living and service.

Pollard: **Your leadership experience is quite varied. Do you remember the earliest days of leadership? What was that like? Right out of Oakwood, as a young pastor, I am assuming. Do you remember those early days, what may have been your uncertainties and insecurities?**

Rock: Actually, my earliest memories of leadership involvement are from high school days. At both Pine Forge Academy and Los Angeles Academy, where I graduated, I was given leadership tasks. There were only five of us who graduated in our class in Los Angeles. I was the class president. But then, everybody was an officer. So we were all leaders. But even before that, in the tenth and eleventh grades the school and church had functions and groups that, in a real sense, were teaching us to lead. Of course, even in younger years, I observed my grandfather, Elder R. L. Bradford, as he pastored several churches in the New Jersey and Pennsylvania areas. Elder Hope Robertson, who pastored our church during my teen years in Los Angeles, often encouraged me regarding a future in church service.

Pollard: **Have you through the years watched leadership change? Have the styles and strategies changed from your earliest days—we may be talking about 40 years of leadership, experience, and observations?**

Rock: I have through the years observed pastors, in particular. But I do not claim to be a guru of leadership styles. All I ever wanted to be was pastor. I never saw myself as anything else. I never had any great interest in other styles, such as the corporate kind. The science of leadership itself never really absorbed my thinking.

Pollard: **Well, you mentioned corporations too and leadership, and one thing is clear today: that corporations are really taking this diversity issue very seriously. I attend a lot of conferences, and they have whole divisions now that are devoted exclusively to diversity. Especially as we go into the twenty-first century. Why do you think this might be so? What implications do you see it having for our church, which is a global church?**

Rock: The mixture of races and groups means that we either learn to get along or suffer from tensions and all sorts of social conflict and loss of resources. There are numerous biblical and altruistic reasons for diversity. But even beyond all that, there is just plain pragmatism. Good sense dictates that if we are going to survive in this society on this planet, amid these challenges in this church, we had better learn how to get along.

Pollard: **You and Dr. Behrens [the president of Loma Linda University] have worked together for a number of years, and back in the early nineties you took on what was then a fairly bold venture of the creation of an office devoted to diversity at Loma Linda University. In retrospect, what were some of the factors that you saw that precipitated the creation of this office?**

Rock: My first encounter with diversity tensions at Loma Linda occurred in 1969. I was pastoring at Ephesus [in New York City] when Leroy Reese, now a member of our board but then a student, called me and, along with several other Black students, requested that I come to California to assist them in establishing a Black student association. They also asked the help of Frank Hale in this matter. I was surprised that they called me. Frank's status, on the other hand, as an agent for social change had been well established in his work with various social organizations within and without the church, and by his role in engineering the election of the first Black General Conference vice president, F. L. Peterson, at the General Conference of 1962. I had assisted in the civil rights struggle during the early sixties while pastoring in Orlando and Miami, Florida. But that was on a rather local scale. And I wondered why the Black students thought that I could be of help? But then I finally decided it was the news of my having obtained a master's degree in sociology at the University of Detroit that gave them some hope in my being able to assist. Frank and I came out, and we were successful in negotiating with the administration so that the Black student movement was established and a scholarship and revolving loan [fund] of about $100,000 (quite a bit at that time) was put together. And that was my first brush with diversity needs here at Loma Linda. The institution has come a long way since then, thanks to the sensitivities of board members and administrators and the hard work of your predecessors, Drs. Garland Millett, Gaines Partridge, and Delbert Baker. However, minority needs for social, financial, and even academic support remain and have suggested the current office that you occupy.

Pollard: **Diversity, by its very nature, is inclusive and largely takes in all groups, but when it comes to education, we are talking primarily about two specific groups of under-represented minorities, Hispanics and African-Americans. What do you envision as we move into the twenty-first century?**

Rock: I think the broader diversity effort is good. I think it is fair. Hispanics cannot be left out of this effort. However, on the chart of social distance, Blacks occupy the bottom. So while diversity is fair for everyone, Asians included, the informed administrator and an informed public should understand that Blacks have needs that no other group has, except perhaps Native Americans—the American Indian. There are several indices that show that the majority of America has boundary-maintaining mechanisms that are more severe for African-Americans than others, including Africans who wear their national dress, and African Caribbeans, who speak with such delightful accents.

Pollard: **How do you ascertain whether an individual is ready for cross-cultural leadership?**

Rock: You do so by noting such traits as courage to risk in relationships. This includes a genuine love for people and the willingness to think and function outside one's ethnocentric or cultural box. It also involves the ability to refrain from bitterness and bias because of negative encounters or impressions. One cannot stereotype an entire race or group because of the distasteful ways of a few. But one must have not only good attitude and affability; one should have attractive and effective work habits and talents as well. These include research capability, writing skills, and speaking ability.

Pollard: **What would you say to the next generation of young people? You have been involved with youth all your life and all your career; you have been very positive toward young people. What would you say to the next generation of young people about to inherit a church that is more multicultural, more multinational, probably, than it has ever been and growing? What counsel would you offer to them? Black young people or young people in general?**

Rock: I would say, be comfortable with multiculturalism; be comfortable with cultural pluralism. Marry whom you wish; go to school where you wish; enjoy the garden variety of humanity in whatever appropriate ways you desire. Don't be afraid to branch out. But on the other hand, don't neglect the challenge to work at the problems within your own ethnicity community. I believe that the major focus of minority social concern should be that of fixing and not mixing. Social mixing is legitimate and can be enjoyable and should be natural. But that should not be the primary goal of social action. The biblical principle of starting in Jerusalem and then branching out to other parts of humanity should be kept in mind.

Pollard: Now, let's just talk for a moment, before we close, about how persons can begin to do what you just described— mainly to work, to make a contribution to their community, to like who they are, to know who they are, and then to move on and to also be available to make contributions beyond. Now . . . let's talk about the nature of identity. I have tried to argue that diversity competency requires first and foremost that you come to grips with who you are as a cultural being.

Rock: That is correct.

Pollard: Why do you think that is so?

Rock: If you are negative about who you are, you will probably resent others and/or be challenged with feelings of inferiority. Either way, one suffers in terms of communication. To be successful, the diversity endeavor must be advanced by individuals who are not ethnically threatened. The nonthreatened person can be open and honest about his or her own or group's weaknesses and needs while at the same time working to overcome biases or restrictions imposed by dominant groups.

Pollard: And with that I think we will stop. Is there anything else you would like to say?

Rock: Only that while the monetary pay given for leadership in the Seventh-day Adventist Church does not always equal what one might receive in some other communities, the rewards—spiritual and psychic—are far more satisfying than money. So that a person such as I, born in Harlem, reared in southwest Los Angeles, who never dreamed that he would ever see any other part of the world, can come to my present career stage and look back in amazement upon God's leading. There is something about our message, our educational system, our denominational culture, that inspires and equips for service and hence leadership at both laity and clergy levels. I am happy that the truth found my family long before I was born and that I have been allowed a small role in the advancement of the gospel.

INTERVIEW WITH B. LYN BEHRENS, M.D.

President, Loma Linda University;
CEO, Adventist Health Science Center

Interviewer: Leslie N. Pollard, D.Min.

Vice President for Diversity
Loma Linda University, Adventist Health Sciences Center

Pollard: Today, Dr. Behrens, we are talking about leadership and diversity, and we would like to begin with a few questions. Where were you born and reared and educated?

Behrens: I grew up and had the preliminary part of my professional [training] in Australia. My home was in Cooranbong, New South Wales, which relates to Avondale College. I stayed there until I went to Sidney University to do my medical education and then did two and a half years of residency in Sidney before I came to the United States. Subsequent to coming to Loma Linda to do pediatrics, I have had training in Atlanta, Chattanooga, and Denver.

Pollard: In what capacities have you served here in Loma Linda?

Behrens: I was the first pediatric resident on this campus in 1966-1968, and then came back on faculty in 1970 for two years. Then in 1975 I came back as a faculty member in the Department of Pediatrics and ran the Pediatrics Residency Program, then became vice chair in the Department of Pediatrics, moving from that into the responsibilities as the dean of the School of Medicine and then president of the university.

Pollard: Is there anything about that process you would say . . . has prepared you for the leadership tasks that have come to you?

Behrens: Yes, on several counts. Leadership, in general, is the ability to take data, aggregate it together, see your options, choose the best of the options, and then implement. That is the whole approach to collection [of] symptoms and signs, analyzing [them], making a diagnosis, and then implementing a treatment plan. But beyond finely tuning those analytical tools and then implementation . . . comes the imperative that medicine is a discipline for the majority of people who interface with people. And so your ability to be effective as a clinician is very much dependent upon your ability to get cooperation from your patients. A glamorous or well-articulated [or] well-designed treatment plan is useless if it is not implemented. And the person and people who have to implement the plan are, in fact, individuals whom you encounter for only a brief period of time, and then they go back into their own environment, and they have to either choose to do it or not to do it. So finding ways to communicate and motivate are an essential role of a successful physician. And that, of course, has direct implications in it for leadership.

I think the second way that it impacts is particularly relevant to Christian leadership. And that is having a philosophy of life and a view of life that cause you to keep your spirituality integrated with your profession rather than isolated and walled off from it. And in my beginning days in being the dean of the Medical School, a realization dawned on me that has only grown through time, and that is that Christ's life is a model for how to be a health professional. Not in miracle-working, but as a human interfacing with human beings. Going to the values and virtues of that interaction of compassion, dignity, and respect, etc. And through the years, that understanding of Christ as model has expanded into Christ as educator and, most particularly, Christ as leader. And that, to me, sets the stage for what I believe is Christian leadership which is not hierarchical and top down, but a sense of being called to hold up everybody else and to make their work effective and efficient and meaningful in the pursuit of mission.

Pollard: **So your philosophy of leadership really reaches back to the example of Christ. You mentioned the interpersonal components of that leadership. What does this mean for diversity?**

Behrens: It is my view that we are enriched and [that] collectively our pursuit of mission is enabled by the blending together in a team of diversity of talents and backgrounds and perspectives, united by the mission and building upon a foundation of commitment to excellence. So rather than my having a sense that I have to have all the answers and know all the details of the direction and being the only one that God works through, my sense is that God empowers all of us and that if we will work together and move down the path together, God will empower a team of people. And so personality differences, talents, backgrounds, [and] perspectives become an essential part of teamwork.

Pollard: **How did you come to your understandings about diversity, and—I guess I could ask the second question—why were you willing to put leadership capital behind diversity?**

Behrens: Well, I think as long as I have been supportive of diversity, I have not considered it to be a program, but to be a reality. I have seen us become a global community. I think I started realizing that before I left Australia, where there was a very large emigration thrust in the late fifties and sixties. And Loma Linda moved from being a very uniform society, with very homogenous backgrounds of people, into a very diverse society, which it continues to be. My sense [has] amplified since I have been in the United States, particularly in southern California. Someone has to be blind to not recognize that there is huge diversity in the United States. The question, then, that immediately flows from that is, How does one take diversity and create an incredible opportunity for [a] society of individuals out of that? And that goes then into the values of fairness, justice, and recognizing that talent and expertise isn't a genetic, racially determined issue, and that particularly in health care, oftentimes people from the same racial and ethnic background better serve the people of their same background. I think the practical example moving it from just generalizations to specifics [occurred when] I was a young faculty member at Loma Linda. I had a child who had very severe asthma, [from]

162

a Hispanic family, and I could not get any cooperation with this family. This goes back to what I said earlier, [that] you make a diagnosis and you need to develop a wonderful treatment plan, but if nobody takes and implements it, it is useless. I was in the clinic one day and was seeing this child with very uncontrolled asthma. I had a young medical student with me who was Hispanic, and I [had] just walked out of the room and had expressed my extreme frustration about the lack of progress in this child's illness. He asked if I would mind if he went back in and tried to help the family understand why this was really important for them to follow through. That was the turning point in that child's illness. So a medical student's ability to communicate went beyond speaking Spanish. It went into linking it to traditions, family values, all the things I didn't know how to hold together to help them understand that this was important and how it worked. This child's health was improved because a Hispanic medical student worked with me that day, and it was a turning point in that child's life until I finished caring for him.

Pollard: **As a leader of a global organization, what is it like being the first female president of Loma Linda and the first female . . . president of the Medical Center?**

Behrens: You know people occasionally ask me that question, but it is not one I have thought a lot about. So I have always experienced throughout my entire professional life—with one exception, and that didn't happen here—a sense of equality with my professional peers, who were all men, that I have never been conscious of gender differences. When I became president, there was so much that needed to be done and so few of us to do it in the pursuing of the mission at the university and improving its well-being that each of us took a piece of it and were trusting each other, holding hands together, figuratively, and just saying, God has called us to do that at this time and we will, with His help and empowerment, and in working with each other, achieve it. So there has always been an orientation around mission and not about our differences, which I have found very invigorating. I think this same thing has happened in the Medical Center. I have had the privilege of working with wonderful men and women, God-fearing people, who are extremely talented and who are not stinting in using their talents for God. Really, I just don't know what else to say except that it is a very exciting and creative environment [in which] I have been privileged to work.

May I tell you an example when it didn't work? Many years ago I worked in another state and another facility during my training years. In working in that place, for the first time in my entire career up to then and subsequently, I really didn't feel connected to the person who was my supervisor. I struggled and struggled with whether it was based upon my open affirmation of my faith, that I would not attend teaching rounds or conduct teaching rounds on Sabbath, although I would work with patients and work as hard as anybody else in the care of the sick; but I would not use my Sabbath time in terms of educational enterprise. I wondered if it was because we were so different in our perspectives, and I wondered if it was a gender issue. I was an immigrant from Australia, and he was an immigrant from the Middle East. So I didn't know if it was a social background issue or a gender issue. I left that one-year experience, marking it down as I don't know, but wondering if perhaps it was gender difference. Probably 20 years later, while I was dean of the School of Medicine, I had a phone call one day from this gentleman, who had learned that I had become a dean, and he called to apologize. His apology was that he had not treated me appropriately. So I was not just being overly sensitive. He went on to explain that [that] particular year in my training he was facing board exams and, recognizing that I was quite competent to handle the entire service, he had dumped on me and basically gone off to do his own study and left me to do all the work. If he had only told me that he needed to do that, I would have gladly picked up the whole load and helped him. But by keeping me in what I felt was abandonment and abuse from the point of overwork and nonsupport was interpreted by me in many other ways that were not right. So I think beyond that experience of misinterpreting people's actions, as I did, it also speaks to the imperative of communication. So don't try to jump to conclusions.

Pollard: **When you think about leadership now going into the twenty-first century, do you think leaders need any special skills to go into the [next] century, where we are increasingly leading across cultural lines, and if so, what would some of those be? You have mentioned one—communication.**

Behrens: I think that the degree of specialization that exists within the world and the complexity of our modern world dictates that one can work in teams. In many regards, it is like the family doctors of yesterday have been replaced by the "sub-sub-specialists" of today. And so we can do more today because of that sub-specialization and still connect to the generalists. I think it is imperative to recognize the complexity and not to have any sense that you need to know everything, you [must] make all the decisions; but rather to recognize that a team of people bring the expertise together, multiplying the effectiveness of the team. So [the] ability to work [in] teams is a crucial skill for the twenty-first-century workplace.

Pollard: **What else do you see, in addition to communication and the ability to work in teams?**

Behrens: Clarity of mission for the leadership team and simplification of mission. I think that the more one can simplify what the essence or bull's-eye of what one is doing, the more united your team will be about doing that. Then you fan out from that, radiate out from . . . the application of that mission, and grasp the opportunities that keep floating by. I think another . . . imperative is to have clarity of values, and taking those values from a philosophy statement into everything you do in your organization and how you interface with those you serve. The clarity of values is threaded through policy and procedure, threaded through expectation of behavior, threaded through the evaluation process. It should undergird the entire organization and be the fabric that is woven together in a tapestry and expresses itself in so many ways.

Pollard: **Could you share with us a value from Loma Linda and**

how that works its way through the organization?

Behrens: Compassion. And I think of the values that any organization can have; a health-care organization that does not have compassion as its number-one priority will eventually turn into nothing but a business.

Pollard: **Compassion versus what?**

Behrens: Materialism. Compassion versus profit.

Pollard: **OK, compassion is consistent with what we are trying to do here?**

Behrens: It means that . . . for the people who make the institution come alive through their work each day, . . . one needs to have standards of performance. But the way one upholds the standards of performance is done graciously and gently, in treating people with dignity and respect, and in being able to recognize when brokenness has entered into the life of someone and try to help them try to find healing through that, even as one does not diminish the expectation of excellence. The compassion that a patient feels.

Pollard: **What makes a hospital a Christian hospital?**

Behrens: A hospital is more than [a] place; a hospital is people. It is the people who come for care and the people who provide the care. It is [that], from my perspective, a Christian hospital is not in health care; it is in health-care ministry, which means [that] when one addresses the physical or emotional dimension of someones brokenness, one doesn't see them as a disease, [one] sees them as a person. But beyond seeing them as a person, [one] sees them as a person who has the dimension of spirituality, and so that in all of that sometimes it is just by the loving way that a person is cared for. But at the right time and the right way, as did Christ, implanting those little seeds of hope and faith in the souls of people so that they might, in fact, spring up and be fruit for eternity.

Pollard: **As a leader, you have the reputation of listening well. What are some of the keys to doing that?**

Behrens: [One is] not trying to formulate your own philosophy and response without really hearing and understanding. I think really being present at the moment of the communication. I really think trying to understand what the message is and then, before you rush to respond to it, even spend time clarifying what that message is so that you are sure you really understand. Somebody today was saying, not to me, how cultures talk past each other, and I'm not sure I am understanding where you're at, but if I am understanding where you arc at, then this is how I would respond.

Pollard: **Lyn, when you think about leadership, how do you approach people's ability to learn leadership?**

Behrens: Leadership is lifelong learning. Just as in any profession, one needs to be continuously learning. Leadership is the same way. Refinement of all the skills that it takes to be able to effectively move an institution forward is [not only] in the secular learning, but . . . in the principles of leadership, which are so beautifully exemplified in Scripture that it is a study of a lifetime.

Pollard: **You mentioned Scripture. [One] of the mottos that you have lifted up before us as an administrative team is servant leadership. Tell us what that means to you.**

Behrens: The image that is always created in my mind, or the vision [that I get] when I think of servant leadership, is Christ kneeling and washing the feet of Judas. And when one puts that in the concept of the Deity, the ruler of the universe, who knew the future and knew not only that Judas would betray Him, but that Judas was His betrayer [and] would and could do that. So whenever one is challenged as a leader, or whenever one is demeaned, misrepresented, which are the hurting parts of leadership, when our best intentions are ill spoken of, one has little to complain about when you think of Christ's examples. The other thing, too, is the gentleness that night with which Christ, who could have really moved from a motivation of love to a motivation of fear if He had [wanted to], handled Peter . . . where He warned him, He told him to keep praying. . . . He allowed Peter to suffer the consequences of his lack of following guidance, but was still loving when He turned and looked at Him in Pilate's hall. There are so [many] servant-leadership implications in that encounter in the upper room that are food for thought and really set a measure of servant leadership that is so far beyond anything that I could imagine myself. It has to be a journey.

Pollard: **Do you think women lead differently than men do? I am talking about group differences, not individually.**

Behrens: I think about in all my experiences with men [to] whom I [have] reported—and I have always reported to a man—I've been blessed with collaborators, and so I hear it reported to me that men are so much more authoritarian and directive, and women are much more collaborative. But I have been blessed by a stream of collaborative men whom I have worked with, and [they] have treated me with dignity and respect in equality, and [to] whom I never felt afraid to express my opinions and views. And I felt valued.

Pollard: **I'm wondering how much of what we hear about gender-based leadership differences is stereotyped?**

Behrens: I've been a professional now since 1963, and when I think about all the interchanges that I have had in 36 years, I can't imagine that they don't know I'm a woman. [Laughter.]

Pollard: **One last question, Lyn, and that is for young people, as you are a person who also really reflects a commitment and an advocacy for young people. Is there anything that we can say that would help them be more effective in a multicultural world?**

Behrens: Well, I think the things I have said before are not to be negated, but the symbolism I carry in my mind is that of the cross with the vertical dimension; [that] is the imperative of my daily remaining connected with God. And the horizontal dimension is with equality, reaching out my arms to embrace others and help them, and that really is the symbol of wholeness with one's care and concern for people in all the dimensions, and the ability to be a channel of God's love to those we interface with.

Pollard: **God created diversity. We heard you say that the other day. Any parting words or thoughts that you would like to share with our audience today?**

Behrens: I just think we have an incredible opportunity [in] a world where we stand at a point of time with unparalleled opportunities. . . . So here we are being called, having the opportunity of living in an age of unparalleled knowledge and technology and materialism. We live in a time when the values of the kingdom of heaven have never been more challenged than they are today, all set in and packaged in the . . . packaging of society's acceptance. So you have, by contrast, the calling that we have as citizens of the kingdom of heaven to live in vulnerability to each other. At the same time there has been an ever-burgeoning self-centered culture that almost eclipses Christ from people's view.

Pollard: **Thank you, Lyn.**

INTERVIEW WITH HYVETH WILLIAMS, D.MIN.
Senior Pastor, Campus Hill SDA Church
Loma Linda, California

Interviewer: Leslie N. Pollard, D.Min.

Vice President for Diversity
Loma Linda University, Adventist Health Sciences Center

Pollard: Tell us a little about your background, educational preparation, and how did you learn about leadership?

Williams: I don't know where to begin. I was born in Jamaica, grew up in England, and have lived most of my life in the United States. . . . I have a really diversified accent because I have a little bit of each place that I have lived in. Most of my education was in the United States, and I just finished last year my doctor of ministry degree at Boston University and am preparing for law school right now. I am studying for the LSAT. It is not over yet.

Pollard: Now, today, on the diversity front, leadership and diversity in the twenty-first century are inseparable in the globally connected world. Corporations have taken this diversity concept seriously.

Williams: The whole political system of the United States is talking diversity. The number one question that the candidates are being asked right now: What will your cabinet look like if you become president? And the ones who say "Like me" are out. That is the big picture.

Pollard: Why do you think corporations are taking diversity seriously?

Williams: That is where the world is now. This global thing is not just a map with people in different places, but an integral coming

170

together of a variety of cultures and people. *Time* magazine did a cover story on what America would look like in the year 2000. Not one of them was totally Black or totally White; that was their prediction. So tell me diversity was here and it is here, and I am glad that we have finally awakened to the understanding that America was never a melting pot; there will never be any melting pot or salad bowl or whatever. Because diversity allows us to be who we are and yet share and honor and experience the authenticity of others, it is beautiful.

Pollard: **You are leading a church that is clearly multicultural. What is it like?**

Williams: It is wonderful, and you need to know that this is intentional because I am not sure that Loma Linda was ready for it. It just didn't happen. The moment they decided to call me here, I saw an opportunity because I am a very significant showpiece for diversity. Being female, being of color, being of another culture—all of these things come into play. So when this church called me, being primarily White Caucasian, . . . to be their senior pastor, I said, "Hey, they are ready." I took that as a statement of readiness.

Pollard: **Did you and the Campus Hill church need to discuss diversity?**

Williams: No, I didn't need to discuss it because they called me and I assumed it, so I moved and I began to set up an organizational structure, such as having pastors of different nationalities, and that is deliberate. We do not have a worship service where there is only one group of people, men or just women, or Blacks or just Whites, or young or just old. It is a mixture in my worship service, and we deliberately do that.

Pollard: **Your platform reflects that too.**

Williams: Yes, we plan that every week, and I did that in Boston, too, so I had the experience [of] already implementing that in Boston. In downtown Boston, where they'd had the biggest race riot, we had a multicultural, diverse congregation that people used to just come in and enjoy. I had families who drove two hours from New Hampshire and Maine and said they wanted their children to experience this because this is the real world.

Pollard: **You had people driving from across state lines?**

Williams: Yes, because this is the world they would have to function in.

Pollard: **Now you are in a multicultural congregation, I guess there are values conflicts at times, but my observations are that we have values contrasts rather than conflicts.**

Williams: It depends upon the leader.

Pollard: **What would you say are some of the primary values of your base culture? Describe your base culture, then the values, and how . . . they help you in terms of a multicultural setting.**

Williams: I would say that I am from Jamaica, and my understanding and perception and belief about the Jamaican people is that we are a very mixed group of . . . nationalities. We had class problems, not racial problems, and that is very important to know, because you could have a poor White person who was badly treated and a rich Black person [who] was treated well. It was class, not color, in the West Indies. That is a very important distinction.

Pollard: **When I come to your church, your spiritual passion is clearly a culturally born and nurtured quality. It is clear that in terms of multicultural ministry, your passion for God impacts this congregation.**

Williams: But the good thing is that it is giving permission to all these other cultures who want to do it anyway, to say it is all right, and that is what diversity does. It not only brings in other resources that we lacked, but it gives us permission to be more

172

profound and expressive and to be real.

Pollard: **As a female pastor you came into a male-dominated ministry, and really, most consider you and a few others some of the real pioneers. The younger women now who are going into ministry will never have it as challenging as you did. What was that like?**

Williams: People have ripped broaches off my dresses, . . . smacked me in the face, and they have done this in God's name. But the good thing is that Jesus told me that they would do this. Had He not whispered that in my ear, I would [have been] totally unprepared for it, but He did say that there will be some who will do this in My name and say they are protecting me and doing it for my sake, and I am telling you this so that when it happens you will know how to behave.

Pollard: **Tell me now, as a woman, what do you think women bring to what had been a males-only . . . ministry?**

Williams: I think that you are going right into the heart of my theology here. I believe that if God created us both male and female in His own image, a male-dominated ministry gave a wrong concept of who God is, and therefore, though it did many good things, . . . I can show you in the Bible that . . . God allowed it to happen; I am not sure that He set it up. But it is written in the Bible that it would be so, that the ministry would be male-dominated until these days. It is very clear in the Bible, because Joel 2:28 says in the last days . . . women would come into . . . ministry. . . . We are in the last days, so you are going to see more and more women, until it is a balanced ministry, until we begin to show the full picture, the full image of God.

Pollard: **So women in ministry provide that complimentary aspect of ministry?**

Williams: Now, there are some who believe that there are things that women can't counsel men [about] and this sort of thing, and when I travel, people, especially male ministers, will ask,

"Well, how do you counsel men, and do your head elders and deacons listen to you?" Well, it reminds me of when the world believed that a Black quarterback could never run a team. I remember that because I am an avid football fan, and now they are out scouting every Black kid who holds a ball over their heads. It is a myth, this idea that leadership has to do with one's culture or color. Leadership has to do with one's understanding of the role and the responsibilities.

Pollard: **What else do women bring to the ministry?**

Williams: One of the main things that people have missed that women bring, and I think that when more women are brought in, it will be seen, [is that] there are not that many fights in the churches where women pastor. [Laughter.]

Pollard: **Why is that?**

Williams: Board meetings arc not . . . I don't know why it is, but I think that we don't feel as challenged, and so if someone disagrees with us, we don't have to put up our "dukes" to prove our power; we have other ways of getting to the point (laughter). We are peacemakers, reconcilers. The very strength of women is connectedness; we don't like to be disconnected from anything or anyone, so what we bring is connectedness. And so I have had, in all of my churches, groups of people who absolutely did not like what I did, and instead of me getting in their faces or something like that, or so that it divides the church, I quietly say to them, "I will nurture you and treat you with respect, but if you are miserable here, please find another place to go, where God will use you. You are still my brother or sister, but we don't have to stay here and fight, because fighting is not our game, and I don't need to make you agree with me. I will respect your difference."

Pollard: **You preach to lots of different cultural groups, multicultural audiences. Do you do special preparation based upon [those to] whom you are going to speak? And if so, how do you do it?**

Williams: Let me answer that question in two parts. When I first started out in ministry and I was invited all over the world, I did that, and I would leave that situation feeling like a hypocrite. An example is the first time I went to Australia. That is where I decided, "I am not going to do this anymore." The first time I went to Australia, at the opening [meeting] there were maybe about 5,000 people, Sabbath morning there were 15,000, I am told, who came to the sports arena, and at that time that was the largest group to whom I had ever spoken. . . . The Friday night meeting was young people, and as I started trying to reach the Australian White young people, I was not going anywhere. I remember I was up on the big screen sweating bullets because I am not making any connections. I see kids walking around, leaving. I am just not connecting, and I just said no more, I am being fake. And right there I just looked out at the people and said, "Here is who I am," and I got down and they got up.

Pollard: **Tell me this, what do you think are the most important skills, then, to being an effective multicultural leader? There is a point where we have to make some adjustments, but there must be some skills we can identify short of being untrue to ourselves. Like Paul did.**

Williams: If you are untrue to yourself, you are out of the game. People sense that. I think the number-one key to multicultural ministry or diverse congregations is to be who you are. I remember one day not too long ago I was preaching, and I said something about rhythm and everything. I said, "I have to show you people how to have rhythm, because we, my people, we have rhythm. Even if I can't use it, I got it." Do you know, the only complaint I had was from a Black person who said to me, "I am so sorry that you feel so badly about yourself that you have to make an issue about your race." And my interpretation of . . . why I did that was because my congregation and I have come to the place where they know I am Black. If they don't know by now, something is wrong, and I am so comfortable with them that I can say you White people, and if they say you Black person, it is no big deal because

175

it is not racism; it is just that we have broken down the barriers in Christ and we are talking real, and we don't have to formulate it, to articulate—we just say it. So then the number-one key is authenticity. Know who you are; reflect on who you are; accept and admit who you are.

Pollard: **Is it true that some people can't do multicultural ministry because they are really in denial of who they are?**

Williams: Absolutely. It is just like, I wasn't born and raised in church, so I have partaken of the world. If I deny that, then I am no longer capable of ministering to unchurched or churched people because I am being pretentious, I am lying, and anything else that comes out of my mouth, why should they believe? And you know I understand it, because years ago when I was in Britain and I was in the entertainment industry, you know, I used to do acting and modeling and all these sort of things, [and] you could never get me to admit that I was Jamaican. I spoke with a Cockney accent; in fact, to this day I refuse to do it because it brings back memories of the fake days. There are people who say to me, "How come you don't speak with a Cockney accent? I spoke, I learned, and that was the only way I spoke, because I would never admit I was a Jamaican. . . . So because I was dealing from that false place, everything in my life was built on falsehood. Therefore, I had nothing secure in my life.

Pollard: **How can we reach our desired maturity in diversity as leaders?**

Williams: By effort. We need to emphasize that because the effort is like driving a car. When I first started learning to drive, I was glad nobody had video cameras on me, because I was jarring my way to every stop sign. Every stop sign that I stopped at I knew; now I drive anywhere in the world and I stop at stop signs, and I don't even think about it. Why? Because now I am an experienced driver and I trust myself at it.

Pollard: **How is diversity like that?**

Williams: Diversity is like that in that in the beginning there are some spots of awkwardness, and you see everything you are doing because you have to be intentional; but keep on doing it because one day it will be just like the breath that comes out of you, it will be the sweat that comes out of your pores, it will [be] so natural, and we just have to [be] intentional in every phase of our lives until it becomes natural, until it is as we breathe. Until then, no one is a good practitioner of diversity.

Pollard: **Say something about multinational congregations. I hear people say, "We have 25 nations represented in our church; that is diversity."**

Williams: That is political diversity. But relational diversity—that is not it. It is when I can have in the privacy of my relationships anyone of any culture or color. That is when I begin to practice diversity. Whether I marry them or not, until I can break down those barriers of distrust, then I am not there. One of my favorite stories I heard in Boston, and I have told it over and over again: I went to a Martin Luther King, Jr., breakfast, and one of the guys there, this priest, told this story of a rabbi who, I am sure you have heard it or read it, asked these kids when is dawn, "Can you tell when it is dawn?" And one of the students got up and said, "Is it dawn when we can look up on a hill and see that a tree is not an olive, but a fig?" And he said, "No, that is not dawn yet." And another student said, "Is it dawn when we can look in the early morning hours, when the mist is just clearing, and see two animals in a field [and know that] one is a fox and the other one is a wolf?" And he said, "No, that is not it." And they said, "Well then, what?" And finally he said, "Dawn will come when you can look in the eyes of a brother or sister and know that that person is your brother or sister. That is when dawn comes." . . . When there are no barriers at all.

Pollard: **Thank you very much.**

INTERVIEW WITH ELDER NEAL C. WILSON
Retired President
General Conference of Seventh-day Adventists

Interviewer: Elder Ted N. C. Wilson, Ph.D.

President, Review and Herald Publishing Association

TNCW: **How long have you been a worker in the church? In what capacities have you served?**

NCW: It has been my happy privilege to serve the church for about 60 years. Fifty years as an active paid worker and 10 years as an equally active but unpaid worker, with an office in the General Conference [building] and an efficient secretary for two days a week. My first denominational job was as assistant to the treasurer of Vincent Hill School and College in India, then as an accountant in the Southern Asia Division Office. [Following that I was] acting treasurer of the Oriental Watchman Publishing House; assistant cashier at the St. Helena Sanitarium and Hospital in California; pastor-evangelist in Sheridan, Wyoming, and in Cairo, Egypt; health, public relations, and religious liberty director of the Central California Conference; and health and religious liberty director of the Columbia Union Conference. I was given the opportunity to serve as president of the following organizations: the Egypt Mission, the Nile Union Mission, and the Columbia Union Conference; [then] 12 years as president of the North American Division, and 12 years as president of the General Conference of Seventh-day Adventists. In addition, I have served as chair of many educational, health-care, publishing, radio-television, humanitarian, and other boards of directors. The past 10 years have been busy with many special assignments: such as offering advice and counsel, reading manuscripts, serving on about 10 or 11 different boards, chairing various committees, and doing considerable work in the area of mediation and reconciliation, besides serving as an elder and Sabbath school teacher in our local church.

TNCW: **Tell us about the impact that you think your service has had on your family.**

NCW: It is evident to me that my family has been the source of enormous support and [they have] identified themselves with many of my responsibilities. This experience has caused them to become acutely aware of what we would call "servant leadership," which actually means that a person is available at all hours of the day and night to serve others. They have fully recognized the fact that in a leadership role one cannot take sides without knowing all available facts regarding a given issue, and then one must deal with principle rather than with personalities. This all leads to the extreme need for fairness. It has helped my family to establish respect for all regardless of ethnic background, linguistic differences, age, color, and sex. It has also helped my family to know that one cannot become engaged in sidelines or use an office or authority for personal benefit or for personal gain. They have realized and understood the demands of church leadership and have become valuable participants in serving Christ and His church.

TNCW: **Would you do anything differently as you look back on your leadership?**

NCW: Perhaps I would have tried to spend more time with my precious companion and children. Perhaps I would have not been so willing to accept new and additional assignments. Perhaps I should have focused more rather than being a generalist and open to every and all demands. Perhaps, if I had to do it all over again, I might have kept a more accurate diary and put some more effort into writing.

TNCW: **Do you remember your earliest days in leadership? What were they like?**

NCW: It became necessary to spend much time on my knees talking to the Lord and in gathering accurate information. I quickly came to the realization that I needed to follow God's formula, which is to do the very best you can under the ministry of the Holy Spirit, after getting the best counsel you can, and leave the rest to God. When I went home, I turned off the business and the tensions of the day. One cannot afford to lie awake at night and worry and develop ulcers. When you go to bed, one needs to be thankful for God's promises and the evidences of His leading and the success that He provides. I quickly learned to be patient and resourceful, and it also became essential to stretch money as far as possible. When facing formidable challenges, one must always remain calm and convey a sense of positive trust and assure people of God's tender care for His church.

TNCW: **How did you learn about leadership? Did you have mentors?**

NCW: My education in leadership and administration came largely from watching and listening to my father, who, during my life, was president of four local fields, four unions, and four world divisions. In other words, I grew up in the home of a recognized leader and administrator. I discovered that there was virtue in being known for being long-suffering and decisive and respectful of others. My father and the Holy Spirit were my mentors. I was taught to keep my eyes open and look for those who loved our message and mission, and who had the potential of being winners. Something which I learned early was that the greatest challenge to a leader is to help others succeed and become potential leaders.

TNCW: **Can you describe a time when you felt most challenged as a leader?**

NCW: It is difficult to confine my answer to one situation. To illustrate, there were many times when it seemed that we had the Red Sea before us and with no easy way of escape. When the Suez Canal crisis developed, all United States citizens were asked to leave Egypt, and my family was among them. I chose to stay and identify with our people and to make sure that fear and the threat of an invasion did not divide our church. We had no idea whether we would be reunited as a family again, but we believed that God had sent us to Egypt and that we needed to shepherd our people. Another great challenge which I faced was to get official recognition in Egypt for our church and its humanitarian activities. With God's help, this was achieved. In the mid-eighties it became apparent that certain influential internal forces in North America were determined to split the church. There was also an abortive attempt to discredit Ellen White and to undermine and weaken the faith of God's people in her prophetic gift. In the early eighties it was imperative that the credibility of the Advent message be established in the Soviet Union. This is a great story of divine intervention in human affairs. A challenge of international proportions has been how to train and develop competent national leadership. The Lord has helped this church to make a significant switch from expatriate to highly successful national leadership.

TNCW: **Corporations are taking diversity seriously. Why do you think this is so, and what implications does diversity have for church leadership?**

NCW: One of the complicated concerns that we face in almost every part of the world, is how to reach the full and hitherto unrealized potential of fulfilling the gospel commission. It is important that each worker feels his or her true worth and value. The dignity of every individual must be a prime target. We must be positive in accepting the reality of diversity and the importance and advantages of multicultural leadership. As a result of communication, transportation, e-mail, computers, distance learning, teleconferencing, etc., our world is shrinking. Education and training are becoming universal. We must strive to become one world family and recognize the enormous significance of comprehending diversity. The Seventh-day Adventist Church must not fall behind in enthusiastically endorsing and promoting multicultural leadership. There are untold opportunities. We must see people as people and recognize that our international family is growing rapidly, and therefore, we need to involve as many as possible in leadership responsibilities. The times we live in urge us to listen to the counsel of the apostle Peter, where he says that we should be like one big happy family, full of sympathy toward each other, loving one another with tender hearts and humble minds. It is imperative that we realize that we belong to each other and each one needs all of the others (1 Peter 3:8). The apostle Paul, in Romans 12, appeals to us to work happily together and not try to act "big." Don't try to get into the good graces of important people, but enjoy the company of ordinary folks, and by all means, don't think you know it all. This is how the appreciation of diversity helps us to weld the world family together as a unit.

TNCW: **What do you believe makes a person an effective cross-cultural leader?**

NCW: Paramount in cross-cultural leadership is having one's heart filled with the love of Christ and a love for every single child of God. We must look at each other with respect and must never underestimate the possibility of an individual regardless of their background. It may not be easy, but it is essential. Once you have determined what you want, then you can almost assume that that is what they want. I learned an invaluable lesson and philosophy of life as a boy in Central Africa, where all my playmates were African boys and girls. We had different cultures, spoke different languages, lived in different homes, ate different food, looked different, but we all ultimately wanted to be loved, to be educated, to be successful, and to be recognized and earn dignity and self-worth.

TNCW: **You are widely seen as a leader who is effective in leading across multicultural lines. Is there special preparation or research that you do before communicating with a multicultural group?**

NCW: Much prayer, much humbling of heart, much effort to search for data and history of issues that may arise. I have tried to understand human beings and always to be careful not to use demeaning terms or illustrations. I have endeavored to look for, and learn from, models of successful people from different cultures and backgrounds. One of the greatest achievements is when one can be seen by others as genuine and totally sincere. It is my opinion that . . . people of other cultures simply need a chance to demonstrate their capabilities, their natural talents, and their commitment to excellence. This is why it is never wise to talk about any particular national or cultural superiority or inferiority. There are different approaches, different views, and different opinions, but this is not to say that one is necessarily superior or inferior to others—only different.

TNCW: **What values in your own culture are similar to or different from those you serve? Has your base culture taught you anything about leadership? If so, what?**

NCW: This is an interesting question, because frankly, I have never been quite sure of my own culture. I grew up in so many different places and was exposed to various cultures, historical backgrounds, languages, etc., that I was very positively influenced by each. I unconsciously identify with many cultures. As a boy I listened to the folklore of the African elders sitting around a village fire. In India I gathered the wisdom of many centuries of history and culture. These things became a part of me. I came to realize that character was the greatest and scarcest virtue that exists. True character comes only as Christ is able to mold a life. I was the product of many cultures, all of which merged into the person that God has helped me to be.

TNCW: **What can we do to prepare the next generation of leaders for effective multicultural leadership?**

NCW: Example leadership is the strongest and most powerful teacher outside of the ministry of the Holy Spirit. We must model what we know to be right. The teacher must be what he or she expects the student to become. We must not live a double life. Remember that a life is, after all, the most powerful evidence.

TNCW: **If you were mentoring a new leader, what skills would you tell her or him are necessary to lead across multi-cultural lines?**

NCW: If we become reflectors of Christ's character and become true followers of the Master Teacher, and if we will take time to learn from many cultures and backgrounds, and read the counsels of Ellen White, especially the last four chapters of *The Ministry of Healing,* we will certainly come close to achieving God's design. Remember that racism is a moral issue, not simply a social issue. True cross-cultural appreciation and an understanding of the blessing of diversity come only to a life that has been converted by the grace of Christ.

INTERVIEW WITH RALPH S. WATTS, JR.

President,
Adventist Development and Relief Agency (ADRA)

Interviewer: Leslie N. Pollard, D.Min.

Vice President for Diversity,
Loma Linda University, Adventist Health Sciences Center

Pollard: **Could you tell us about your background and the work of Adventist Development and Relief Agency?**

Watts: Well, my background is [that I have] grown up in an overseas environment, having been born in Korea, educated in China, and then [returned to Asia for 13 years, during which I have covered the entire Asian region, six countries, and experienced] very diverse cultures, languages, and religion. Working in that environment, I believe, helped me develop a sensitivity to the uniqueness that we have as a church organization. . . . I have felt that those years spent living and working in [an] international setting have helped me considerably [in my] work [at] ADRA [in] dealing with government [and] church leaders in every corner of the globe.

Pollard: **So your experience of growing up in an international setting benefited you in your work. What kinds of insights did you gather, in reflection now, as you grew up in a non-American setting as an American? What kinds of insights did you gather that have helped you in your work today?**

Watts: Well, I think that it helped me to realize what it was like to be a minority and obviously in a country where everyone . . . has black hair, dark eyes, and then to see a blond or brown-haired individual with blue eyes walking around—I stood out. I think that type of experience has enabled me to be sensitive and to be careful and not [be] patronizing or offend those who are different than I am, but to appreciate what they bring to the table. There is a great deal that can be learned when we work with people of different cultural backgrounds. Having had that background, I think, has made it easier to adjust, to work within cultures without creating a lot of uneasiness for myself or for those whom I work with. Our office staff here at headquarters is multicultural. The executive vice president of ADRA is from Chile. We have leaders here from Africa. We have leaders from Asia. We are working in a multicultural setting right here in headquarters, which is the way it should be. We are a microcosm of the worldwide church.

Pollard: **What do you think diversity brings to an organization?**

Watts: I think that diversity brings strength to the organization. If you don't have it, how can you truly call yourself an international organization? Any international corporation would be well advised to have at the management level leadership that reflects the clients whom they are going to work with.

Pollard: **I would certainly agree, and increasingly in our church, too, we are becoming more conscious of diversity issues.**

Watts: And second, I think that it is incumbent upon these corpora-

185

tions to utilize their financial resources to get the training and the development of their personnel. As they work in this kind of environment, they should be looking for potential leaders whom they can develop and bring along and move into major positions of responsibility as these positions open and as they have developed qualifications to fill those positions. I think that there is a twofold prong that needs to be looked at in this regard.

Pollard: **In the twenty-first century, where increasingly we are [looking to be] more globally connected than we have ever been, what would you say are the skills that are needed in order to really be effective in this multiethnic, multicultural, multiracial environment that all leaders find themselves working with today?**

Watts: I think that it is extremely important to look at the qualifications that an individual brings, not as necessarily the culture or the color. What we really need to focus on is the fact that this is an individual whom God has endowed with special gifts, with a unique background, with an environment that may be different from mine, but still that individual can bring something to the table that is unique, that will blend in and complement others who are on the staff. That is what needs to happen. There is a special quality that comes from the uniqueness that we have as individuals. That is God-given, and as leaders we need to see that, accept it, build on it. And by doing so, then we will affirm each other and we will be benefitted because we are building on the strength that comes from the diversity that we have.

Pollard: **And of course, [as] you were one of my presidents in the early days of my ministry, we saw you do that in the southern California area.**

Watts: Yes, we did. We had 33 language groups, 60 different countries [represented]. I enjoyed that. I did not feel threatened by that. I enjoyed it immensely. We would get into a meeting with the workers [and] have the give and take and the fun.

We had a good time, and there is no reason why people have to feel threatened in that kind of environment.

Pollard: **How would you assist our leaders on every level [to] become much more comfortable in working in a multicultural [environment]?**

Watts: We should not as leaders become defensive; we should not try to build walls around us or our so-called own little wicker cane that we may have. Let's open up communication; let's engage; let's get involved; let's spend time together, pray together; let's fellowship together, play together. And as we enter into this kind of interpersonal relationship, a lot of these barriers will come down. That is what has to happen, and I think that is the kind of environment that I wanted to create while I was in southern California, and I think to some degree it was successful.

Pollard: **Sometimes we . . . gave you a hard time, didn't we?**

Watts: It was fun, and you guys got a chance to blow off a little steam. Leaders have to allow for that. It is important for leadership to allow for the younger leaders to vent some of their frustrations without reacting negatively or defensively, or saying, "Oh, man, I am not going to put up with that kind of stuff." You have to get beyond that. A leader has to get beyond that and say, "Hey, look, this is a part of growth, it is a part of maturation, it is a part of understanding who we are and what it is that we have that we can contribute to the success of the organization." I think that is very important for leaders to understand.

Pollard: **Now, let's say that a person has the qualifications now for a position in a multicultural setting. What do you think are some of the skills that make for success as leaders work cross-culturally?**

Watts: I think the ability to negotiate and to find ways of communicating when difficulties should arise that seem to preclude any kind of satisfactory solution. There are going to be times when we come face-to-face with a situation that just defies a simple solution. Many of the problems that we are dealing with today are very complex, and there is no simple answer sometimes. Some of these crises, some of these problems, some of these challenges that we face, simply do not have a simple answer, so we have to spend time gathering the best brains that we have in a rational and in a Christlike spirit [to] try to resolve these issues by taking sufficient time to analyze and to look for the appropriate steps that need to be taken, and many times they cannot be done in a quantum leap. The best way to solve a lot of the issues that we are dealing with today is in incremental steps. We need to set an objective or a desired goal that we are striving for. Let's just say, 10 years down the road, this is the way we would like to see the church or our institution look, and this is what it is going to take to reach that, but we are going to have to do it on an in-cremental basis and then review the progress that we are making periodically to see whether or not we are heading in the direction that we wish to go.

Pollard: **So then, one of the skills that is really essential is the ability to negotiate?**

Watts: Yes. And vision also.

Pollard: **Would you agree that [the problem of] working cross-cul-turally is intensified because now we have people's sen-sitivities, their expectations, their self-images, and other factors influencing perception? Does that sound fair?**

Watts: I think there is no question that the way you deal with major issues in southern California are going to be far different from [the way] you deal with [problems] in Bangkok or Seoul. So you are going to need to look at the uniqueness of the culture in which you find yourself. Then there needs to be competent representation, not emotional, but calm, reasonable leaders who can come to the table and say, "This is a problem that we all have to deal with; let's find a way of working together and resolving this issue." [We need people who will] ask, "What is the desired outcome? What is it that we really want to . . . accomplish here?" Then we should back up from that objective and begin to develop action plans and appropriate steps to bring [about] that desired outcome. It may require human resources; it may require time on the part of pastors, teachers, medical people, whoever, to bring about the desired results that you wish to have. The diversity presents a complexity, but there is a strong benefit when we have stakeholders as owners, players, in resolving . . . the issues. Then from the conference's standpoint, what resources do you need from us, what kind of human resources do you have available, what steps can the churches take, and so forth?

Pollard: **Elder Watts, we watch you go in and out of all of these different cultures. Here I am in my little town in Kansas, or in my little village right on the outside of Bangkok, and I am in a local church. How do I begin [to] exercise competent leadership across cultures? I may never get to where you are, but in my little local arena, whether it be in South America or in Asia, how do I begin to take my first steps toward being cross-culturally competent?**

Watts: I think the first step would be to try to assimilate, as much as you can, an understanding of that culture. For me, it is living, working, eating, traveling, associating, with people of that particular culture. I think that is extremely important. If I want to try to understand a culture other than that of my own, I need to take the time and the effort to try to better understand what it is that is unique to that particular culture and what are the strengths of that culture. Every culture has strengths, blessings that can come to the body of the whole from the variety of cultures that we have. It is a wonderful thing that we have this. It makes this world an interesting place to live and work and travel [in]. Why do people travel, why do people like to go overseas? I like to travel because I like to be in an environment where there is a different culture. For me that is not intimidating; that is invigorating. I think that is what an individual needs to do. Adaptability is another point. You need to be flexible and adapt to that culture where you find yourself. When I visit Black churches I love the culture that comes through. I love the music; I love the preaching; I love to see the expression on the faces of those visitors who are sitting on the front row. I feel comfortable with the difference, and you will find my foot tapping to the beat of the music. I am also comfortable in Japan, where they are sitting there going through their liturgy . . . bowing. It is a totally different culture, but I love it because it is different. When I worked in Southeast Asia as president of the union I had six hospital boards, and they were in different countries. When I was in Vietnam, the Vietnamese were more emotional, more expressive. They were quick to laugh, and they were quick to cry. They were quick to forgive. That is the Vietnamese culture. When I was dealing with the Vietnamese on board meetings or committees, you understood that, and I knew how to relate to that. Then I got on the plane and flew 40 minutes west to Bangkok. Now, the culture in Thailand is totally different. The people are more reserved; they are much gentler, they are loving, and they do not get angry quickly; they do not express emotions rapidly—it is sort of kept within. So when I met with leadership over in Bangkok, the board members and others, I had to make a change in my mind. I got on the plane and said, "OK, now I have to switch gears a little." You have to adjust yourself to the environment. It is incumbent upon leaders to be able to develop the ability to be . . . comfortable in any environment in which you find yourself. If you are in an area and you want to understand people, the only way you are going to do it is to get in there and spend time with them. Read about the culture. Try to understand people. Talk to them. Develop friendships with them. Eat their food. Go to their cultural events, and then you will understand and appreciate what it is that they have.

Pollard: **Thank you very much for sharing your thoughts.**